The Scandal of God's Forgiveness

The *Scandal* of God's Forgiveness

Edmond Smith

RESOURCE *Publications* • Eugene, Oregon

THE SCANDAL OF GOD'S FORGIVENESS

Copyright © 2017 Edmond Smith. All rights reserved. Except for brief quotations in critical publications or reviews, no part of this book may be reproduced in any manner without prior written permission from the publisher. Write: Permissions, Wipf and Stock Publishers, 199 W. 8th Ave., Suite 3, Eugene, OR 97401.

Resource Publications
An Imprint of Wipf and Stock Publishers
199 W. 8th Ave., Suite 3
Eugene, OR 97401

www.wipfandstock.com

PAPERBACK ISBN: 978-1-5326-3616-5
HARDCOVER ISBN: 978-1-5326-3618-9
EBOOK ISBN: 978-1-5326-3617-2

All Bible quotations, unless otherwise quoted, are taken from the English Standard Version, Crossway Bibles, 2004.

Manufactured in the U.S.A.

To Kerryn, my devoted wife and soulmate, who patiently typed up *The 'Scandal' of God's Forgiveness*, and who inspires me in love for our precious Lord and Savior.

"Come, my Joy, my Love, my Heart:
Such a Joy, as none can move:
Such a Love, as none can part:
Such a Heart, as joyes in love"

—George Herbert, 1593–1633

Contents

Introduction | ix

Forgiveness through the Eyes of Israel (1) | 1
Forgiveness through the Eyes of Israel (2) | 7
Redemption in Matthew | 12
Redemption in Mark | 19
Redemption in Luke | 21
Redemption in John | 28
Redemption in Acts | 50
Redemption in Romans | 55
Redemption in 2 Corinthians | 63
Redemption in Ephesians | 69
Redemption in 1 Timothy | 75
Redemption in Titus | 82
Redemption in Hebrews | 85
Redemption in 1 Peter | 91
Redemption in 2 Peter | 94
Redemption in 1 John | 100
Redemption in Revelation | 106
Conclusion | 110

Bibliography | 113

Introduction

IN THE 1950S, WHEN it was not unusual for songs of a Christian theme to appear in the Western world's hit parade charts now and then, a song simply titled *He* captured considerable attention on the radio. It carried the refrain—

" . . . Though it makes Him sad to see the way we live,
   He'll always say, 'I forgive.'"

Many took to recording the song and faithfully sang the refrain as the composer intended but George Beverley Shea, the famed singer for the Billy Graham crusades, took the liberty to rephrase the refrain, so rendering it as

" . . . Though it makes Him sad to see the way we live,
   He's always *ready to forgive*."

In line with Billy Graham's approach to evangelism, it was clear that George Beverley Shea was anxious in the light of Christ's death to highlight how divine forgiveness is conditioned by a sinner's willingness to repent, that a sinner cannot be freed of the consequences of the guilt of sin unless he or she first repents. Doubtless Shea sought in song to correct a common notion that cheapens God's forgiveness, whereby people are not regretful about sin itself and may only be seeking to avoid the consequences of it all, without desiring in earnest to amend their ways. Does not biblical repentance mean to "change one's mind" and stands for a conscious turning away from evil with the sincere intent to fall in line with the holy ways of God? There are people who expect God to change his mind without them changing theirs for the better.

It is good to be reminded that repentance is required to secure divine forgiveness, but we can overlook the matter of the divine prerogative when it comes to forgiveness. What of forgiveness from God's point of view? Is it possible that while "he's always ready to forgive" despite the acts of the grossest of sins, we overlook that it lies in the prerogative of God as to whether or not he forgives? None deserves divine forgiveness. Forgiveness essentially is an act of divine mercy. Can it be said that repentance earns divine forgiveness? If we regret offending God and seek his pardon, do we then earn forgiveness and, to put it perhaps crudely, force God's hand to pardon? Or, could it be that no-one in his natural state seeks forgiveness and is under the sentence of death, imprisoned while awaiting the sentence of death, and that essentially and solely he depends on "His Majesty's Pleasure" as to whether or not he shall be released from condemnation? Could it be that not all who are subject to imprisonment and who are deservedly awaiting the sentence of death are destined to be released?

Legally in the secular sphere a person may be released from the penalty of a crime that he has been convicted of when a pardon is granted by an authority such as a king, a president or a governor. A pardon hangs on the prerogative of the authority granting it. It is out of order to question the right of the authority or chief executive in the secular sphere to release or not release an offender, challenging his right to forgive.

When it comes to salvation in Christ, we are reminded of the Apostle Paul's inspired word concerning the imprisonment of all men as "prisoners of sin." Paul says in Galatians that before faith came through the appearance of Christ, we all were "prisoners by the law (of God), locked up until faith should be revealed." He goes on to say: "So the law was put in charge to lead us to Christ that we might be justified by faith." We truly become sons of God by faith, he says. Paul says much about "faith"—that which we ourselves clearly exercise for salvation—but having faith as one who had been "set ... apart from birth" (Gal 1:15) to be called by God's grace. Paul speaks of faith but of a faith required not merely to preach Christ among the Gentiles, but to be saved.

Some claim predestination is merely a call to service and not for salvation. Paul was predestined from his mother's womb to be saved. He could not serve the Gentiles unless he had been saved.

INTRODUCTION

This is the apostle who speaks of us as all people who were imprisoned by sin. Clearly, he viewed any release from imprisonment and condemnation in terms of divine prerogative, telling the readers of Galatia a little further into the letter that it is also preferable to say God now knows us rather than stating that we know God (Galatians 4:9).

If it is true that it is out of order for any in the secular world to question the right of an authority to release or not to release at their pleasure any who are convicted of a crime they have committed, then is it not out of order to question the right of God as King of the universe to release or not to release any who are fallen people and are under imprisonment, any who through sin have been justly condemned for the offences they commit against his majesty? None of us "have done our time" to warrant release. Any release lies in the pleasure of God. It certainly used to be commonly stated in former days throughout Europe that a prisoner's release was not ensured "until His Majesty's *Pleasure* be known." Paul tells also in Galatians that God called Paul by his grace, being "pleased to reveal his Son to me" (Galatians 1:16). God is not obliged to pardon anyone. Not only is it that man in his natural state is imprisoned and bound by sin, but God is free, free to pardon or not. It is a marvel that he pardons anyone. We should expect surprise that any of us are saved. Indeed, Paul marvels at the thought of being saved, and the wonder of it lies in the privilege and the free right that God possesses to grant release and forgiveness according to his pleasure.

While Paul states in Galatians that "Scripture declares that the whole world is a prisoner of sin" (Galatians 3:22), clearly he does not mean that no one was the subject of God's saving grace until Christ appeared, for he quotes Scripture which said of Abraham for one: "He believed God, and it was credited to him as righteousness." He goes on to say: "So those who have faith are blessed along with Abraham of old, the man of faith." Any acquaintance with the Old Testament reveals there were others beside Abraham who had faith and it was credited to them as righteousness before the time of Christ.

By and large those who had such saving faith before Christ were of Israel. Of course, many in Israel did not have saving faith, but by and large it was within Israel that saving faith was uniquely found. When Paul writes that the whole world was a prisoner of sin before Christ came, he refers to the whole world in its natural state, the world bringing on itself a deserved condemnation. Yet, saying this, Paul does not overlook the fact "the gospel was announced in advance to Abraham," as well as to others of the race of Israel, Israel being God's chosen and unique people.

That Israel was God's chosen people—saying of them before the times of Christ that "You only have I chosen of all the families of the earth"—recalls the concept of imprisonment and of the pleasure and authority that some were pardoned, released and forgiven, while others remain "incarcerated" deservedly. While the whole world was a prisoner of sin, it was as it were, that in a sense God uniquely placed Israel on parole and gave them out of his prerogative the privilege of knowing him—of being his family. No other people in the world could claim to be in his family. God chose not to include in his family many others in the world outside Israel. Was it not his pleasure to do so?

As King of the universe he had the right to pardon whom he would, with the chance that there could be those who would be released and forgiven. Faith was not to nullify the wonder of it all; since it pleased God to reveal himself to some, faith was then given to them so that they would be released and forgiven. The assuring word of a pardon inspired the human object of God's favor to trust him and then made the release and pardon sweet.

A remnant of Israel was forgiven and released, but surprisingly some Gentiles became the object of God's mercy and were also released and forgiven—the Old Testament makes this plain. We say "surprisingly some Gentiles" . . . because (to reiterate) the majority of those released and pardoned at the time were of Israel. Many in ancient Israel did not have saving faith, but that some Gentiles did at the time does not obscure the fact that God chose Israel to reveal himself comprehensively to the exclusion of passing over most in the rest of the world.

If such exclusion is evident, then it suggests unsurprisingly that once Christ came, God would continue to offer pardon and forgiveness according to his prerogative and pleasure. Although

INTRODUCTION

this thought may seem to be countered by claiming God merely revealed himself to Israel so as to have a nation from which Christ would come—a nation that came into existence merely to serve as a preparation for Christ—it overlooks the fact that the world outside of Israel was passed over by God and was not the object of his saving grace before Christ. Even in Israel herself there was a considerable number who hardened their hearts towards God and became the objects of his anger. In Hebrews the writer says that those of ancient Israel had the gospel preached to them (Hebrews 4:2), which means that outside of Israel in ancient times by and large most of the Gentiles did not have *the gospel preached to them*. Paul in writing the letter to the Romans tells us that apart from the gospel the heathen have no excuse for not believing in God, in the same letter telling us that God, according to his prerogative, hardens whom he wills and has mercy on whom he wills (Romans 9), even with the coming of Christ.

We have noted in passing that when Paul refers to the whole world once being a prisoner of sin, he does not mean exhaustively that not a single person was an object of both God's pleasure and prerogative, and that none therefore had failed to gain pardon and forgiveness "before the time." So we have seen that the reference to "the whole world is a prisoner of sin" was a blanket expression and it ought to caution us against shrouding the term "the whole world" to mean every individual the world over every time that the Scriptures employ the term, or has a term similar to it.

This short book explores what the New Testament teaches about the extent of Christ's atoning death, the very atonement that provides the means by which we have forgiveness in the eyes of God. It seeks to view forgiveness through Christ in terms of God's pleasure, power and prerogative. It seeks to clarify in conjunction with God's pleasure and prerogative what is meant by such terms as "all", "the world", and "many"—the "all", "the world", the "many" for whom Christ died . In short, it endeavors to make plain the scope of God's forgiveness.

We speak of God's forgiveness for eternal salvation. There are two forms of divine forgiveness that ought to be taken into account when we endeavor to make clear what is meant by divine forgiveness for eternal salvation, as forgiveness can either embrace the passing over of a blameworthy action without censure and punishment, or freeing a person of the consequence of his or her guilt.

An example of God passing over a blameworthy action without censure or punishment is cited in Psalm 78:38. Modern translations render the verse in a way that speaks of God being merciful and atoning for Israel's iniquities when they rebelled against him in the desert, while the Authorized Version rendered it –

> "But he, being full of compassion,
> *Forgave their* iniquity,
> and destroyed them not."

The excusing by God of Israel's iniquities was tantamount to forgiving them. A careful reading reveals that he merely overlooked their evil conduct. He overlooked it in the sense that he did not destroy Israel as a nation, but allowed her to move on in the desert. He restrained himself and did not stir up his full wrath (v. 38 again); if he had have stirred up his full wrath, the nation would have been destroyed. Therefore there is an overlooking that may pass as forgiveness. Another example of this is on the cover of a book written by a Holocaust survivor: "I Forgive Hitler." The sins of Hitler are being overlooked by the survivor, though we may be sure that God has not forgiven Hitler in the sense of freeing Hitler of the guilt of his sins and their consequences.

Then there was the kind of divine forgiveness that showed itself in freeing a condemned person of the guilt of his sin before Christ came, when the gospel was known in advance. In one of his confessional psalms—Psalm 32—David tells us of the blessing that could be known in the forgiveness of transgression, in sins being covered, the kind of covering whereby the Lord did not count David's sin against him. David, upon acknowledging his sin before God and refusing to cover it up, found the Lord forgave *the guilt* of his sin. This kind of forgiveness stood in great contrast with that forgiveness God exercised towards his grumbling nation in the wilderness. It is not said that Israel was *blessed* when God forgave her, but that Israel merely did not suffer God's full wrath. It is not said

INTRODUCTION

that God forgave them of *the guilt* of their sin, but simply that he did not destroy them. It is not said Israel confessed her sin so as to secure God's forgiveness to the banishment of their guilt—to the contrary, Israel went on to flatter God with their mouths and lie with their tongues to him instead. When the nation was not faithful to God's covenant, it was a forgiveness that merely overlooked their evil and spared the nation of being exterminated.

In the following chapter "Forgiveness through the Eyes of Israel" we see that the Old Testament also makes plain that God has a purpose of ultimately making Israel a holy nation, as well as bringing forth from among her people the person of Christ who was not only destined to be Israel's Savior but the Redeemer of Gentiles as well, all hinging on the prerogative and pleasure of God to forgive, thus encouraging the Early Church initially in believing that at least the Gospel with its message of forgiveness and freedom from condemnation was for them the Jews.

Forgiveness through the Eyes of Israel (1)

WHEN DEBATE HAS EVER arisen over the New Testament terms such as "all" and "the world" and "many" with regard to the redemption and forgiveness found in Christ, the Jewish perspective is rarely considered. In times past it has been called on at times as a witness to the meaning of "all" and "the world" and "many" whenever the court has been in session about the terms, but even then the Jewish perspective was not fully appreciated, when in fact it plays a significant part in shedding light on the extent on Christ's death and for whom he actually died. Even many of those who espouse the view that God has not forsaken Israel—that He will bring forth a believing nation in Christ from her in the future—fail to grasp or further apply the truth of Israel's uniqueness to the question of the extent of redemption and forgiveness as procured through the death of Christ.

It is essential to appreciate to the full why the apostles of Christ upon his ascension were slow to see that salvation through Christ was for Gentiles as well as the Jews, why Peter for one needed a vision before he realized that the Gentiles would be saved as well. He needed a vision even though Christ is said to have opened up the minds of his disciples to understand the Scriptures so that they could see that it was written that repentance and forgiveness of sins is to be preached in Jesus' name to *all nations*, beginning from Jerusalem (Luke 24:45–47).

(It is a curious way of putting it but Darrel Bock says in his Application Commentary on Luke: "... the disciples took ten chapters of Acts before they saw that 'the nations' mean more the Diaspora Jew." Is Bock suggesting that the disciples first interpreted "the nations" to mean just evangelizing only *Jews* among the nations? It is quite plausible that they thought this way, and that the disciples' understanding was constricted to their eyes only opened to a small and somewhat nationalistic appreciation of what was meant by the necessity of Christ's death and suffering at that point. In whatever way we understand what is meant by the disciples' minds being opened, it took some time before it was realized that the gospel is for non-Jews as well.)

What caused such a delay? Why were the disciples entrenched in the notion their God was God for Israel only? We need to consider then God's clear and particular favor for Israel before Christ came, even though some signs had long beforehand been pointers to the salvation of Gentiles as well.

From the outset it soon became evident that Israel was central to God's plan for mankind. David Dorsey, author of *The Literary Structure of the Old Testament*, claims that from the beginning of Genesis to the end of Joshua is found "an intricate and overarching symmetric scheme" of the centrality of Israel in God's plan for mankind. For after the Fall, as Genesis 1–11 reveals it, peoples of the earth came to live in their respective lands upon the divine overthrow of Babel—all peoples, except the descendants of Abraham. As Dorsey says: "Conspicuous by its absence (in Genesis 1–11) is ...Israel." Then in Genesis 12, in what could be called a lopsided account of things in Genesis, the history of Abraham and his descendants is accorded much attention in the divinely inspired record, until Israel finally receives its own land (Joshua 13–24).

We are to observe then that when Israel has "the rapt attention" of God in the center of the giving out of the Sinaitic Law, Israel is promised upon her obedience to him the status of being God's *treasured possession so that she is to be for God a kingdom of priests and a holy nation*.

Several scholars have noted how vital the text of Exodus 19:6 is, and therefore they see it as foreordaining Israel "to meditate and intercede as priests between the holy God and the wayward nations of the world, with the end in view of not only declaring his salvation, but providing the human channel in and through whom that salvation would be effected" (Eugene Merrill endorsing the view of Walter Eichrodt). While Israel may not have become conscious of her existence for such universalism at the time of the Sinaitic

FORGIVENESS THROUGH THE EYES OF ISRAEL (1)

Covenant, later prophetic writings allude to Israel being groomed for such a universal priesthood, though the struggle to become a holy nation was ongoing. In fact, those prophets with the keenest of prophetic eyes only saw from a far distance the time when Israel would actually be the holy nation, holy enough to possess the pure priests required to evangelize the world. There were prophetic eyes that were compelled to see even beyond the Exile and the Return from Babylon.

Prophets such as Jeremiah, Ezekiel and Daniel looked into the far distance when the nation would only be purified at the appearance of the Davidic Messiah. According to Jeremiah, God would establish with the house of Israel a new covenant that would see God's law put in the hearts of his people so that in reality as a nation at last he was their God and they were his people (Jeremiah 3:31–34). The fortunes of the land would only be restored "as at first" when the Righteous Branch sprang up from David's line, the Branch who would bring about righteousness in the land, at the time when a satisfactory priesthood was established as well (Jeremiah 33:11–22). Ezekiel predicts the kind of return to the homeland whereby the nation will no longer suffer the disgrace of famine, and will see the people with a new heart and spirit (Ezekiel 36:22–32).

Ralph Alexander observes that the return of Israel under Zerubbabel did not see the complete restoration for land and people predicted by Ezekiel. It refers to an End-time Return. Then in Daniel we meet him who is the Son of Man, the Messiah, but who will only prove to be Israel's Messiah and King in full at the End-time. Until Israel is characterized as a *holy nation*—and not merely possessing relatively few godly individuals—will she become a Kingdom of priests. Not merely priests but a kingdom of priests. Israel must have the King Messiah enabling her to reign as a kingdom, and in the authority and power of kingdom-rule that has a holy manner to reach out to the nations.

Now, while much emphasis was placed in the Old Testament writings on Israel's destiny as a holy nation and a kingdom of priests, there also appears in one place or another that which may seem to some a sense of superiority or disdain towards Gentiles when her destiny is realized. For instance, in Isaiah 60 we read of

Gentiles coming to Israel's light in the latter days, and the Gentiles acting as servants to assist Israel in bringing back the rest of her people to the land of Israel. If Gentiles do not serve Israel in any way needed, they "shall perish" and will be "utterly laid waste." Then, in Micah we read that the remnant of Jacob in the latter days shall be in the midst of many peoples "like a lion among the beasts of the forest", which "treads down and tears in pieces, and there is none to deliver." Does this mean Israel will be superior to the Gentiles, with the Gentiles having to serve them, so as Gentiles they do not enjoy a complete reign as Israel will under the Messiah?

Even if such a prophet as Isaiah predicts the Gentiles will seek God with success, and that the Messiah will bring justice to the Gentiles so that their hope is realized in him, will restored Israel lord it over both the converted and the unconverted Gentiles all the same? Will there be a strata in terms of rank when the Messiah reigns?—the saved of Gentile and Jew to the Jews' greater favor?

Does the book of Jonah shed any light on this issue? For it is a record of how God took pity on Gentiles in the Ninevites, when Jonah was loath to have pity on them.

There was a hesitancy on Jonah's part to obey the Lord when he was commissioned to go to Nineveh, even though he was told to "preach against it." He might have been most eager to preach against the very wicked city in order to see it destroyed through its refusal to repent. At a time when Israel (the northern Kingdom) was hurtling to its destruction because of its godlessness, Jonah left his country when it would have been natural to regard those Gentiles as enemies of Israel, yes, just when Israel seemed soon to be given up to Gentile power and destruction. Jonah would have been sensitive to certain self-righteousness in regard to this. It is not far-fetched to believe Jonah was hoping against hope that Nineveh would not repent and thus be destroyed so as to spare Israel of destruction from her. Jonah's initial disobedience reflected not only his own but that of Israel's disobedience as well—with pride in God's election of her becoming a stumbling block against emerging as priests to the Gentiles. That Jonah hoped for the great city's destruction is evident, even though he finally agreed to go to Nineveh. He went "obediently"—under duress.

FORGIVENESS THROUGH THE EYES OF ISRAEL (1)

When God is seen as merciful to such heathen people, Jonah waits to see if their repentance is genuine. When it appears to be genuine, he sulks. It is then that he must learn that God desires to show favor to Gentiles. Through chastisement the prophet's conduct was meant to be such that he desired, like God, the salvation of Gentiles, especially of so many children who were relatively innocent.

So does the book of Jonah shed any light on the kind of future status in salvation that Gentiles are to possess in relation to Israel? It shows God may be gracious and compassionate towards Gentiles, "slow to anger and abounding in love" as much to Gentiles as to those who initially were his elect people. Yet, Jonah as a book reveals little of what some other prophets declared concerning the leading position Israel is to adopt when many Gentiles are saved, and when we are all living under the reign of the Messiah on the renewed earth. So Jonah sheds no light on Israel's future status as the center of the Davidic Kingdom, in the exercising of a unique form of kingship as a royal priesthood, if Exodus 19:6 as a promise is to reach fruition.

With the salvation that came to Nineveh, the experience of Jonah serves as a rare example of salvation to Gentiles before Christ, so that Peter still had to be compelled by a vision to see God's intention to save Gentiles, that is, in addition to saving homeland Jews and Diaspora Jews. Says Keil and Delitzsch: " . . . (the reluctance to seek the salvation of the Gentiles no doubt saw Jonah sharing on his part as the prophet) the feelings and general state of mind of the Israelite nation towards the Gentiles." Keil and Delitzsch as Old Testament scholars wisely speak only of a general state of rejection of the Gentiles by the Jews. There were instances of Gentiles being accepted but acceptance of any Gentile was somewhat of a rarity when God exercised his free will and prerogative in favor of revealing himself almost solely to Israel of the time, for familiarity with God's forgiveness became virtually exclusive to Israel and therefore led to the godly of Israel thinking the Gentiles may well be outside the pale of salvation when their Messiah appeared.

The psalmist of Psalm 130 seeks God's forgiveness and then beseeches Israel to put their hope in the Lord, "for with the Lord there is unfailing love and with Him full redemption", saying also that "He himself will redeem Israel from all their sins." Forgiveness and redemption clearly lay in the reach of Israel, though any godly Israelite knew it was nothing to boast about—it hinged on God's unfailing love for that nation. As for the many Gentiles who were passed by in those ancient days, the withholding of such a worldwide pardon appeared not to be questioned when all mankind was justly condemned by the law of God. If there was any pardon and release from condemnation among any Gentile, then the unpardoned and the unreleased still remain rightly condemned.

Prior to the Apostle Peter's vision, he would not have considered it unjust if God in Christ did not turn to the Gentiles for their salvation. Neither would it have been unjust for God to pass Israel by, except the ancient promises of forgiveness for Israel were confirmed at the appearance of Jesus as Messiah. It was God's intention to save a people of Israel. Yet wonder of wonders! In days when religion was bound up the world over with a strong ethnic character (as Bock observes), through an emphatic vision Peter sees that the God of Israel was prepared to "grant the Gentiles repentance unto life (Acts 11:18)."

Forgiveness through the Eyes of Israel (2)

IF IT CAN BE seen that God exercised his free will and prerogative in favor of Israel before Christ and that the Early Church needed to be "convincingly convinced" before it began in earnest to reach out to the Gentiles, and when as a nation God's ancient people were accustomed to the fact they had been singled out by God to the exclusion of all the nations for his ancient revelation, then with respect to the New Testament use of such terms of "all" and "the world" and "many", as related to the people for whom Christ died, a certain consensus may appear to be reachable by *all* believers regarding the frequent meaning of those terms, irrespective of any view of the efficacy of the atonement.

It may seem that no matter what view may be held about the way we come to salvation in Christ, that for both those who believe that salvation is conditional upon men exercising their alleged natural power to co-operate with God so as to make the death of Christ effectual, and those who hold to the belief that men are incapable of believing unless chosen of God to make Christ's death effectual, the Jewish perspective of simply seeing "the world" in terms of peoples beyond the Jewish nation may seem embraceable to both groups when it comes to defining the terminology of "all" and "many" and "the world."

Yet, those who espouse the view that Christ died only for the elect appear to be the sole champions of what is the Jewish perspective, seriously considering the fact that the Early Church at first comprised Jews only, and evangelized Jews only. Then, she reached out to both Jew and Gentile with the gospel in what seemed to her a most radical step, when once she was enlightened about the command to evangelize Gentiles also.

Is it possible for "free-willers" (for want of a better term and without appearing necessarily demeaning) to embrace the Jewish perspective also, where it is applicable, so that Christ is seen as having died for the whole of mankind? If one believes that salvation is contingent on free-will, and even acknowledges that the term "the world" as the Jews understood the term, can he still hold to the opinion that Christ died for every single Jew and every single Gentile?

However, it appears that "free-willers" treat the Jewish perspective with suspicion. It seems that they suspect that those who hold to Christ dying only for the chosen are seeking a poor escape clause in the Jewish perspective to justify their belief in what has been traditionally called Particular Redemption. Or, it seems like a wrecking ball that destroys the doctrine Christ died for all men. Yet, the Jewish perspective—reducing the terms such as "all" and "the world" to mean inclusively Gentiles as well as Jews in general—is only one of a number of arguments that those who espouse Particular Redemption advance for the doctrine.

John Owen, the great Puritan scholar of seventeenth century England, wrote a monumental work *The Death of Death* in defense of Particular Redemption, and in it refers to how the Jewish context needs to be considered when discussing the efficacy of Christ's death. Owen says there are certain texts where "all" and "the world" are related merely to the breaking down of the division in Christ between Jew and Gentile. He says the Jewish context determines the first type of texts that seem to appear to support Universal Ransom through Christ's death as "free-willers" see it, yet the first type is solely connected to the Jewish perspective in that it saw "the removal of all personal and national distinctions, (that is), the breaking up of all the narrow bounds of the Old Testament."

Even though many may disagree with Owen's view of the design of the death of Christ and cling to the belief that Christ died for every man, and that the redeeming work of Christ can be rendered ineffectual on account of man's so-called free-will, it must be conceded by any right-thinking Bible believer that Owen is correct in identifying certain general and indefinite expressions from the Jewish perspective.

FORGIVENESS THROUGH THE EYES OF ISRAEL (2)

As the reader of the *Death of Death* can see, Owen enlists Jewish context for only one type of texts to support Particular Redemption, for Owen knew that such a perspective does not establish with complete solidity the truth about Particular Redemption. Owen held also that *election* and *predestination* of the redeemed without the obstructing contingency of free-will must also come into play for the complete establishment of what he held as the true doctrine concerning the object behind Christ's death.

The Jewish qualifier may lend itself in a sense to a terminology that is general and indefinite. Yet it is common for those who hold to the autonomy of free-will in man, and who regard Christ's ransom as universal in the sense that he has ransomed everyone, to not only view the use of such a qualifier by the adherents of Particular Redemption with suspicion—they persist in believing Christ died for all by ever stating "all" always means "everyone", and "the world" means "everybody all over the earth."

Yet the Jewish perspective ought to be viewed as more than a limitless qualifier in the New Testament. Even in our western culture 'world' concerning people often carries more than one connotation. We need to enter the Jewish mind when we survey the New Testament. We must view the coming of Christ through Jewish eyes, through the eyes of the race to which Jesus belonged, the race that even found among the formidable disciples of Jesus a refusal or a reluctance to consider the possibility of Gentiles being saved.

This book sets out to weigh up what proves to be a persistent note in the New Testament about the Jewish standpoint mainly, as such a standpoint contributes much to the light of *accumulative evidence* for the case of Christ dying only for the elect.

In summing as to what constitutes the perspective in mind, we say—

A. God has a free-will and has the prerogative to forgive or not

B. Those not released from condemnation, and not forgiven, still deserve their punishment

C. Israel as a nation was the unique object of God's pleasure before Christ came, with the other nations being passed over in justice

D. No-one should question God's prerogative to forgive, whether it is considered before Christ came or after he came

E. It was predicted that Gentiles would come to faith and Paul, who was to be the apostle to the Gentiles, was a subject prenatally of God's pleasure for salvation whereby he became a model of the way Gentiles would also come to faith

F. The Early Church's slowness to see that salvation also was meant for the Gentiles should lend itself to us contemporaries seeing the New Testament also through Jewish eyes; the evangelization of "the world" embraced evangelizing Gentiles; by "world" the Jews meant the Gentiles in particular

G. To interpret "all" and "the world" in terms of Christ's death to mean salvation for every single person, whether Jew or Gentile, is to read into the terminology more than the authors of the New Testament intended

H. Although it appears that it is essentially those who espouse Particular Redemption that allow for a Jewish perspective on the matter of the atonement, it must be conceded that definite election was not necessarily in mind when the above terminology was always employed initially to describe those for whom Christ died, whenever the gospel was preached. All Jews and Gentiles were to hear the gospel as far as possible and, by hearing the good news, "the world" as comprising Jew and Gentile was simply in mind. Such terminology as the "world", strictly speaking, did not have in mind the chosen for whom only Christ died.

I. Still, since God passed over all nations and chose only Israel for his revelation in ancient days, it became evident that God still exercises his prerogative to forgive. The ancient word directed to Moses is taken up by Paul when he contemplates the mercy of God for Jew and Gentile: "I will have mercy on

FORGIVENESS THROUGH THE EYES OF ISRAEL (2)

whom I will have mercy; and I will have compassion on whom I will have compassion."

In the following pages attention is paid to passages in the New Testament where the Jewish perspective should come into contextual play and elucidate our minds about the way to define such terminology as "the world", "the whole world," "all" and "many"—all this as related to election and predestination, to God's prerogative to forgive, as to the subject of exactly who are the people for whom Christ died.

While it would be rare for anyone to question the right of a secular governing authority to grant a pardon for any one offender in a prison, when all may remain condemned and remain justly condemned so as to still suffer punishment and not receive a pardon, among Christians there are those of us who consider it scandalous to think that God chooses some for eternal salvation and exercises his prerogative to forgive them upon sending his Son specifically to die for them only. In the following pages calmly and objectively we need to survey exactly what the New Testament teaches about such things, particularly through Jewish eyes.

Redemption in Matthew

> Matthew 1:21: *"She will bear a son, and you shall call his name Jesus, for he will save his people from their sins."*

WHILE IT MAY BE true that Jesus saves Gentiles as well as Jews from their sins, there is no doubt that in this instance of Joseph receiving a prophecy through a dream about the birth of Jesus to his betrothed Mary, we are to understand "his people" to mean the ethnic people of Jesus: As Jesus was born a Jew, so he was to save those of his ethnic race. Jesus' name also was a Jewish name, thus intimating whom he would save. Moreover Joseph would have understood "his people" to mean nobody but his own people and Jesus' people—those of Israel.

Matthew goes on to relate the search that the Magi made in Jerusalem: "Where is he who has been born King of the Jews?" It is interesting that such a question should be so framed as coming from those who allegedly were Gentiles by birth. Theirs was an acknowledgement that Jesus was to become King of the Jews. Their question or belief endorsed the prophecy concerning a ruler of Judah that would be born in Bethlehem and who would rise to become "the shepherd of my people Israel" (2:6, NIV).

> Jesus' other name of Immanuel at birth stood for 'God with us,' that is, 'God with Israel,' as Isaiah understood it.

R.C.H. Lenski, a twentieth century Lutheran commentator, who generally held erroneously to the term "the spiritual Israel or all believers" wherever 'Israel' is mentioned in the New Testament, in commenting on Matt 1:21 showed how he was not completely entrenched in that opinion by expressing the following: "It is impossible to give a double meaning to 'His people': first the people of Israel, and secondly the spiritual Israel and all believers. The two fail to harmonize. If faith and the actual appropriation of salvation is to be the mark of *laos autou,* then only a small part of the Jewish nation is included in the second meaning." For Lenski "his people" may stand for a small part of the Jews (only believing Jews). However, salvation for Lenski is broader than that, therefore for Lenski *laos autou* here represents believing Gentiles as well as believing Jews. Lenski goes on to contend that Jesus "by delivering (a small number of believing) Jews . . . would deliver all nations." Yet, it is more natural to assume *laos autou* in Joseph's mind applied to the Jewish people alone.

We can state this without denying Gentiles were destined to be saved of their sins as well. The prophecy given to Joseph must be seen through Jewish eyes. It refers to ethnic Israel, even though it may only apply, strictly speaking, to believing Jews in any time to come.

It can also be said that inherent in Matt 1:21 is the doctrine of divine sovereignty in salvation. A sound rendering of the angel's words to Joseph emphasizes *autos*: "He—he alone—will save his people from their sins." Even if faith is viewed as a necessary appropriation for salvation, the foundation of salvation is fundamentally Christ's unique accomplishment in redemption, meaning that faith itself is divinely and graciously given to those favored with salvation, since it is Christ—he alone- who saves his people from their sins. It is divine sovereignty and divine determination that ensures salvation will succeed—"He—he alone—*will* save His people."

> Matthew 20:28: . . . *"even as the Son of Man came not to be served but to serve, and to give his life as a ransom for many."*

Towards the close of Jesus' public ministry, the mother of the sons of Zebedee approached Jesus in the hope of securing the thrones beside Jesus when he gains his kingdom. The other apostles were indignant at such a request, but Jesus speaks to all of them about the need to serve one another, since to be first is to serve. Then Jesus seizes the moment to refer to humble service in the third person ("the Son of Man") as to himself, for he came to serve in a service that would indeed be 'great' (see v.26) through the giving of his life as a ransom for many.

Whatever else may be said about Jesus styling himself as the Son of Man, a close look at Daniel 7 reveals the Son of Man stands in stark contrast to the four beasts which appear first of all in Daniel's dream. The Son of Man by contrast is unbeastlike, both with a consciousness and a destiny of an everlasting kingdom, reigning *with* redeemed men and reigning *over* unredeemed men ultimately and universally. Such a divine rule, one of great authority (v. 25f.), could not be established without the Son of Man serving many by giving his life as a ransom.

Jesus as the Son of Man, and unbeastlike, was to be very conscious of 'the many' when he actually gave his life as a ransom. He died as one for the many. Perhaps we are not meant to press 'many' too much as a disparity alongside 'few' or 'all', since the emphasis is more on Jesus dying as one Man in place of many. All the same, when "ransom" is considered, the "many" stands for a large number to be ransomed by one who alone has the power to ransom.

Barely can anyone suggest "many" by necessity stands for "the majority of people." Universalists may gun for a ransom through Jesus' death being a complete and effectual ransom for all people so that all will be saved, but "many" as a term suggests a restriction of those redeemed.

For the ransom to be effectual, what exactly does "many" stand for? Is it that all the world's people are potentially redeemed but, for the ransom to become effectual in actual fact, faith (contrary to what classical Universalists acknowledge) must appropriate the salvation offered through the ransom? Yet, even among all those who acknowledge the necessity of faith to appropriate the offer made to we sinners, two camps mainly exist: There are those who contend that the offer of salvation via the ransom can be resisted by any person to their loss so that the effectiveness of the ransom rests on the freedom of the human will, while there are those who concede the offer may even be resisted for a time but eventually the divine will prevails and persuades with the result that the actual ransom of any or many is divinely bound to come into effect and not be in vain.

It could well be that the original hearers—the Twelve—understood Jesus to mean by 'many' many merely in Israel, since much is predicted about the ransoming of Israel in Old Testament predictions. Still, whoever is considered the subjects of the "many"—whether Jew of Gentile—the nature of such a ransom remains to be considered.

What exactly was accomplished in Jesus' ransoming? What is meant by a ransom *per se?*

Ransoms always secure release from captivity. When the debt or the payment is made, the captive is free. The debt or the payment does not need to be paid again. Therefore, Jesus ransomed a definite many in mind—with his own dear life at the time of his death—yes, even before they exercised faith in him. Did he not die efficaciously before the redeemed placed faith in him?

Matthew records that Jesus said: " . . . no one knows the Father except the Son and anyone to whom the Son chooses to reveal him," and those chosen are those he had in mind when he gave up his life for their redemption. His ransoming was not wasted, nor was it an act of gross over-payment for those who had not been chosen for the privilege of being redeemed, who will not gain from the cost of Christ's death, and who are to refuse any benefit that they might have gained from it on account of their stubborn will.

> If a ransom is "the securing of the release of a person ... from bondage, captivity ... upon payment," then by nature of what is normally regarded as a ransom, Jesus must have secured the release of many from bondage or captivity as a *fait accompli* when he died.

Actually, Universalists are logical in the sense that they perceive a ransom is effective by its nature and, believing in its natural effectiveness, contend all men will be saved when all are helpless to ransom themselves. Yet, Jesus' ransom is recorded as being only for many, if we may express it that way to any expense of making it appear too restrictive.

The ransom through Jesus ought not to be deemed restrictive or limited, since "many" stand for a large number. "Limited atonement" is somewhat an unfortunate term that has been used historically for the acronym TULIP. TULIP as acronym has an early twentieth century origin and was popularized in the 1930s by Boetner that reflects the effort in the seventeenth century of Dutch Calvinists to help sum up the five salient points of Calvinism that

15

were opposed by the Remonstrants. "Limited atonement" is only a satisfactory term if it is employed to combat what is viewed as the error that Christ died effectually for all people.

> Matthew 26:26–28: *"Now as they were eating, Jesus took bread and after blessing it broke it and gave it to his disciples, and said, 'Take, eat; this is my body'. And he took the cup, and when he had given thanks he gave it to them saying, 'Drink it all of you, for this is my blood of the covenant, which is poured out for many for the forgiveness of sins.'"*

Preceding what is now known as the Lord's Supper, Jesus had announced at the Passover Meal that one of the Twelve would betray him. When one after the other asked Jesus whether or not if it was him, Jesus then said, "He who *has dipped* (emphasis mine) his hand in the dish with me will betray me." The meal in which the bread was dipped was the Passover, originally distinguished from the Lord's Supper. The lamb of the Passover was eaten together with bread dipped in a dish composed of a broth of mashed fruit, water and vinegar. In all likelihood Judas Iscariot slipped out from the company after the Passover part of the evening, ensuring he had sufficient time to carry out his betrayal of Jesus.

Jesus instituted the Lord's Supper on the heels of the Passover (v.26), it becoming obvious that his imminent death would be a fulfillment or a filling out to the full of what the Passover had signified to the Jews down the centuries.

If Judas Iscariot was still present in the company of Jesus and the other disciples when the Lord's Supper was finally commemorated, it is difficult to imagine Jesus saying without discrimination "Take, eat, this is my body" and "Drink of (the cup), all of you,"—when Jesus had already stated of his betrayer, " . . . woe to that man by whom the Son of Man is betrayed", and when he added "It would have been better for that man if he had not been born."

Jesus was establishing a covenant through his death, a covenant embracing forgiveness of sins. It is hard to conceive that such a covenant was being made with a man who would have been better off if he had not been born.

It is to be noted that the covenant was to be established for the sake of those who were destined to receive a new heart from God, just as the Old Testament promise declared. Only if God grants a new heart does anyone enter into the covenant Jesus was to seal with his blood. There was an old covenant—an old covenant that resulted only in old hearts, hearts incapable of desiring to walk in the ways of God. The former covenant was restricted to the Jews, but it had failed because Israel could not keep her part of it. It was prophesied that another covenant that was to be established with Israel would be superior because God would give his people a new heart so that they could not fail to walk in his ways.

> Ezekiel 36:25 says—"*I will sprinkle clean water on you, and you shall be clean of all your uncleannesses, and from all your idols I will cleanse you. And I will give you a new heart, and a new spirit I will put within you. And I will remove the heart of stone from your flesh and give you a heart of flesh. And I will put my Spirit within you, and cause you to walk in my statues and be careful to obey my rules.*"

This was the new covenant Jesus was bringing about by the pouring out of His blood. Forgiveness of sins would pave the way for the many to possess a new heart by the Holy Spirit for obedience to God.

Note that even before Christ came, God told Moses that he would have mercy on whom he would have mercy, so that among the whole chosen race of Israel God chose more narrowly some as objects of mercy, therefore there was an election within an election. It could be said that even under the Old Covenant many were the objects of God's mercy, and not all who descended from Israel belonged to Israel (Rom. 9:6).

> We do not hold that the New Covenant is confined only to God's ancient people. Even though the Old Covenant was exclusive to those people, it is not inconceivable that the New Covenant embraces "many" more people—in addition to the believing of Israel. The New Covenant embraces the many and any to whom God gives a new heart.

The New Covenant is more embracing than the Old in terms of many more becoming subject to God's favor, as stemming from grace overflowing to Gentiles but, if the particularism in favor of Israel was obvious before Christ, there need not be a surprise to learn that God still continues to exercise his own free-will and chooses some, who form many, to be the objects of his sovereign grace according to his pleasure.

It has become obvious down the centuries that not all people—be they Jew or Gentile—are given a new heart by God and thus enter into a covenant with him. When Jesus poured out his blood, he had in mind a covenant to bring about forgiveness of sins. Since that covenant has to do with a new heart to ensure that it is effectual, Jesus' blood was bound not to be poured out in vain. So as the covenant was destined to be effectual, so was Jesus' death.

Redemption in Mark

MARK 10:45 IS VERY similar to Matthew 20:28. Mark's whole account of the institution of the Lord's Supper (Mark 14:7–24) also is very similar to Matthew's account. Therefore, refer to what has been written in *Redemption in Matthew* about the two passages, though a word can be added for further understanding of what constitutes a ransom.

God's ancient people were acquainted with the concept of redemption with respect to persons. The stipulations for what was to be done for an insolvent man in the light of the Year of the Jubilee are found in Leviticus. A poor man may have been forced to sell himself to someone who was an alien and thereby lose his freedom. Unless he became rich again, he was in an utterly helpless state. Yet, one of his brothers, or an uncle, or any other close relative of his clan, could ransom him by buying him back at a price, the price being determined by the number of years remaining until the Year of Jubilee, when he would be automatically set free if no relative had redeemed him before the time.

Some in the Early Church speculated as to whom the ransom by Christ was paid to. Was it the devil? We would not press the analogy of the ransom too much, except to say that the slavery from which the ransomed by Christ are redeemed is an alien state we are in until our redemption takes full effect sometime in our life by placing faith in Christ. Until we are ransomed in full effect, we are in a helpless state and only Christ can deliver us, as only he could afford the cost for it. He has already redeemed the many in mind as a *fait acclompli*. The transaction was of his will alone for the many.

In connection with the years leading up to the Jubilee, note the redeemer knew who he was redeeming. He had the means to redeem, personally knew who he would redeem, and paid the price to release his helpless relative. Does this not speak of Jesus and his ransoming power? He knew who he was going to redeem, and then was prepared to pay the price. The price being paid, the transaction was done. The impoverished believer is set free of his helpless state, somewhat in the manner of what transpired under the Old Covenant.

Redemption in Luke

> Luke 22:19-23: *"And he took bread, and when he had given thanks he broke it and gave it to them, saying, 'This is my body which is given for you. Do this in remembrance of me.' And likewise the cup after they had eaten, saying, 'This cup that is poured out for you is the new covenant in my blood. But behold, the hand of him who betrays me is with me on the table. For the Son of Man goes as it has been determined, but woe to that man by whom he is betrayed.' And they began to question one another, which of them it could be who was going to do this."*

AT FIRST IT APPEARS that Luke contradicts Matthew and Mark by having Jesus state his words about the betrayer after the Lord's Supper was instituted, Matthew and Mark having the words about the betrayal spoken during the Passover, which preceded the Lord's Supper.

Besides John 13 mentioning that the dipping of the bread in gravy (as becoming for Passover practice) saw Judas leave the company before the Lord's Supper was introduced to the disciples, Luke's account can be reconciled with that of Matthew and Mark when we understand how Luke set down the order of events in the way he did and the reason behind it.

It can be argued that none of the Synoptists present a rigid chronology at all times, but psychologically one would think Jesus spoke of his betrayal at the hand of a disciple at the table before he spoke of the culmination of the Passover in the Lord's Supper, otherwise the precious words concerning the covenant that was to be ratified by his blood would have been eclipsed in the minds of those who were to be the beneficiaries of forgiveness of sins through redemption by Jesus' death, yes, when it was crucial in that critical hour to know that God had 'the last word' in what appeared on all accounts to be a tragedy. Therefore, it makes sense to view Matthew and Mark's accounts as chronological while Luke's is not, as the New Testament scholar Hendriksen maintains.

Why then did Luke place the words concerning the betrayal at the end of the pericope to do with the Lord's Supper? There is good reason to believe that once Luke presents the account of the Supper, he then straightway demonstrates what total reaction among the Twelve there was to Jesus and his teaching, just as William Hendriksen in his commentary on Luke reveals. There is first the strongly implied reaction of Judas Iscariot (vv. 21–23), then that of the Twelve (vv. 24–30), followed by that of Simon Peter (vv. 31–34), lastly of the group as a whole (vv. 35–38). In this sense Luke's account can be reckoned as 'orderly' (see Luke 1:31).

The plea is that it is unlikely that Judas Iscariot participated in the Lord's Supper, both from a theological point of view (see my comments again on Matthew 26:26–28) and from the view of the construction of the Synoptic texts, as well as that of John. Weight for this can also be perceived in the inclusion of the longer Greek text for Luke 22:17–20, as it is found in the ESV Bible. Presuming the longer Greek text is preferred, it is difficult to conceive Jesus said "This is my body, which is given *for you* (emphasis mine)," if he had already declared the damning words about it being better that Judas Iscariot had not been born.

In fact, such a *personal* assurance and application as "This is my body, which is given for *you*" and "This cup that is poured out for *you* is the new covenant in my blood" is not as common as one may think when the New Testament is considered. Yes, we meet such general expressions as "The Lamb of God which takes away the sin of the world" (and we have yet to seek the full meaning of such in this work), and as for a personal application of Christ's death, it is only ever restricted to believers.

The Early Church message was always to the effect Christ died for sins, or Christ died for sinners. The lack of practical personal application of Christ's death did not discourage any from believing in the early days, as there

---

Never do we read that the Early Church's evangelism was based on the appeal "Christ died for *you*."

was sufficient encouragement to believe in Christ, simply because Christ died for sinners, so conviction could arise without stating "Christ died for you." When one was "cut to the heart" about Christ's death, then one felt constrained to repent and believe, as happened at Pentecost. Therefore, it would have been incongruous for Jesus to say to Judas Iscariot, "My blood is being shed for you," these words only being applicable to the remaining disciples who believed that he held the key to salvation.

Moreover, according to the New Testament no-one is ever said to be condemned on the grounds that he or she was rejecting the death of Christ for them. Rejection of Christ is said to be grounded in refusing to believe in him, and indeed it may carry the rejection of the notion of the cross, but only in spurning the necessity of the cross to save. Unbelief and disbelief spurns the idea that our sin is of such a degree that Jesus' death is vital for salvation. It is essentially the failure to trust him, to doubt his word, to disobey about the need for him to die that incurs condemnation.

Condemnation of sin even exists without having heard the gospel, and without hearing of the death of Christ. Then, having heard of the gospel and of Christ dying for sinners, it is the failure to believe in the necessity of the cross that brings on a greater condemnation.

> Luke 23:34a: "And Jesus said, 'Father, forgive them, for they know not what they do.'"

In the second edition of *A Textual Commentary on Greek New Testament* by Bruce Metzger (1994), the comments are made on behalf of the Editorial Committee of the United Bible Societies' Greek New Testament to the effect that these words of Jesus, upon being crucified, are probably not part of the original Gospel of Luke if we regard the absence of these words from good early manuscripts as being "impressive", but it is said that they bear "self-evident tokens of its dominical origin." It is held that those early and divergent witnesses of excellent and trustworthy manuscripts would not have led to these words being deliberately excised from Luke's Gospel on the grounds that they suggested the prayer of Jesus had remained unanswered, for the fall of Jerusalem in 70A.D. was considered to be proof that the Jewish nation had not been forgiven of God.

Why then were they excised? Metzger does not offer an answer. They were more than likely deliberately excised in some circles on the grounds that the nation had not been forgiven—presuming forgiveness was not understood as simply overlooking their sin, but as freeing the nation of guilt and the consequent condemnation. The Fall of Jerusalem was seen as casting doubt on the authenticity of Jesus' plea for forgiveness.

The NIV bears a footnote to explain that some manuscripts omit Jesus' words for forgiveness, yet the NIV includes them in the text of v. 34—believing them to be originally authoritative enough to retain them.

If the words are authentic and actually had fallen from the lips of Jesus, how are we to understand them? Was it a prayer for the Jews alone? Was it for all who crucified him, both Jews and Romans? What was meant by "forgive"?—how closely does "forgive" need to be defined? Was the prayer in any way actually answered?

Unsurprisingly, quite a number of views had been held about the prayer. Some say Jesus' prayer was simply answered by his death, which made forgiveness of sin possible. That in itself does not satisfy others, among whom are those who claim that Jesus' plea precisely had in mind the Jews who, it is said, unlike the Romans, did not comprehend the magnitude of what they were doing in crucifying him. Others say that the wrath of God on the Jews was not immediately unleashed on them through Jesus' plea, a forgiveness of a kind came in the form of a moratorium for forty years, thus sparing the Jews until the fall of Jerusalem. Forgiveness is then viewed as being restricted to a delay in punishment, and not forgiveness in terms of salvation.

As noted elsewhere (refer to the introduction of this book), there is some truth in a certain forgiveness being a delay of punishment *per se*, or as a pardon pertaining only to physical preservation, or a certain overlooking of sin to achieve a divine purpose. When Moses made tablets for the Ten Commandments, he sought the Lord's presence for Israel, even though they were "a stiff-necked people"; he asked God to "pardon our iniquity and sin", so that

Israel could fulfil the divine purpose of the nation making it to the Promised Land (Exodus 34:9). Psalm 78 tells of God atoning for wicked Israel in the wilderness, meaning that he did not completely destroy her as a nation (v. 38f).

Still, is this what Jesus had in mind when he prayed? And is it true that "He does not define narrowly those for whom he prays"? Scholars who consider the whole of Luke's writings—Acts as well as the Gospel—are on the right track by finding the prophecy of Isaiah for Israel fulfilled: " . . . He bore the sin of many, and makes intercession for the transgressors."

On the basis that textual critics are more often right than not by accepting as an axiom that "difficult sayings" were more likely to have been original than otherwise, they encourage us to believe that Jesus' prayer may well have been authentic.

Metzger does not apply the aforementioned axiom to Jesus' words here—not offering on that basis a reason for their inclusion in Luke—but he could have. Recall that Metzger's reason for regarding the saying as the actual words of Jesus stems merely from believing that they "(bear) self-evident tokens of (their) dominical origin." If this as well proves convincing, the logion lends itself to buttressing the conviction that it is authentic as arising from two sound propositions of probability and preference for a difficult reading in textual criticism.

Now, if the words are authentic, then the prayer was certain to be answered. Christ was bearing the sin of many—not for all but for many, all the same—when He died. And the intercession of "Father, forgive them for they know not what they do"—is to be linked with him bearing the sin of the many.

Certainly, the "many" included those of Israel who were to experience salvation, just as Luke makes clear in Acts. It was more than overlooking or passing over sins in Israel—it was freeing them of the guilt of having crucified Christ (see Acts 2). This is not to say that initially Jesus did not bear the sins of Gentiles on the cross, and did not make intercession for them as well so that they would be saved, but the record of Acts surely defines the most definite subjects of Jesus' prayer in what may seem to some a somewhat obscure request.

Acts records what Jesus continued to do and to teach as by the Holy Spirit (Acts 1:1), so that we ought not to be surprised to learn how Jesus' prayer takes full effect after the outpouring of the Holy Spirit. On the Day of Pentecost Peter is found preaching to a Jewish audience who is accused of crucifying and killing Jesus at the hands of the Romans (Acts 2:23). Could they be forgiven of such a heinous act? Becoming convinced that Jesus is now proven to be Lord and Christ by his resurrection, through the power of the Spirit they plead with Peter: "Brothers, what shall we do?" Peter replies, "Repent and be baptized every one of you in the name of Jesus Christ for *the forgiveness of sins*" . . .

Peter further enlightens us about the nature of the sinful act of crucifying Jesus as committed by Jesus' own people when he has another opportunity before an audience of them to urge them to repent. As Acts 3 has it, Peter once more accuses his own people of Israel of killing Jesus when Pilate had decided to release him. Then Peter goes on to say: "And now, brothers, I know that you acted in ignorance, as did also your rulers." We could also say that the Romans acted in ignorance, but Israel's ignorance was much greater and more serious, therefore it can be safely said that Jesus had in mind his own people when he prayed "Father, forgive them for they know not what they do." Peter offers hope if the people are to repent—forgiveness for what they had done, and the hope of the return of Christ from heaven upon repentance. Since Israel has not yet repented over the centuries as a people, Christ has not returned. Jesus' prayer on the cross has only been partially fulfilled. Yet there is every reason to believe it will be completely fulfilled. His prayer cannot fail to be answered for his ethnic people.

Then, the authenticity of Jesus' prayer is very much confirmed when we learn of Stephen praying "Lord, hold not this sin against them," upon being stoned by the hostile Jewish unbelievers. There is every reason to believe that he was inspired to pray as he did

---

We read that about three thousand of the Jews, who crucified and killed Jesus at the hands of the Romans, believed and were therefore forgiven for putting Him on the cross.

because Jesus had prayed an identical prayer for his and Stephen's people, a petition bound to be answered.

Actually, Stephen's prayer confirms that Jesus' prayer was authentic and that it is to be viewed as an original part of the Lucan Gospel. It also reminds us that even though the people of Israel were largely responsible for Jesus' death, and the unbelieving among them killed Stephen as well, their sin will not be held against them, otherwise their King (Christ) will not return. This is not to say every Jew will be saved. It simply means a far greater number of them are destined to repent in readiness to welcome their King upon his return from heaven, in answer to his prayer for forgiveness.

Redemption in John

> John 1:29: *"The next day (John the Baptist) saw Jesus coming towards him and said, 'Behold, the Lamb of God, who takes away the sin of the world'."*

IN THE LIGHT OF much of what we know about John the Baptist, of the twelve disciples of Jesus and their lack of insight into the salvific nature of Jesus' death as based on the Synoptic Gospels, it appears surprising to read of John the Baptist exclaiming that Jesus was the Lamb of God, who would take away the sin of the world. It is particularly surprising if it is assumed that the Baptist understood what he was saying by his exclamation in the light of what we now know and understand since the resurrection. Don Carson puts forward a case for believing that the Baptist had in mind a warrior Lamb of God as based on ancient Jewish texts, so that Jesus was expected to come as a warrior lamb in putting to flight sin through judgement and destruction rather than by expiatory sacrifice. Either the Baptist understood something the Twelve did not know in advance (see Westcott's *Saint John*), or, the Baptist shared the Twelve's initial ignorance concerning Jesus' expiatory sacrifice (Carson)—so that it could well have been, like Caiaphas the high priest, the Baptist spoke better than he knew. Still, it is not difficult to perceive what John, the writer of the Gospel, understood by the Baptist's exclamation.

It is what the Evangelist understood by the Baptist's announcement that occupies our thoughts—that of the salvific nature of Jesus' death. Whether we consider that its prefiguration was the substitution that was implied in the Passover and had its beginnings in the escape of Israel from Egypt or the sacrificial lamb as depicted in Isaiah, it is pertinent to the subject of the 'scandal' of God's forgiveness that the search be made to comprehend what is meant by the Lamb of God taking away the sins of the world. Will all sin be taken away because Jesus is the whole world's substitute, even to the degree that no person will ultimately have to bear the consequences of their sin? What is meant by 'the world'?

The sacrifice of God's Lamb represents a certain efficacy, with the Lamb vicariously slain for others who are powerless to effect the removal of sin through a sacrifice of their own. And whether we consider the substitution implied in the original Passover or in the prophecy of *Isaiah*, it is evident that the Lamb of God was destined to suffer a sacrificial death for sinners at great cost to himself.

Yet, such a costly sacrifice could not be contingent on a mere offer of deliverance without such a deliverance being complete and sufficient in itself, that is, before one turns to Christ in faith, the atonement has been a fait accompli. The transaction has already been done. We do well to marry the Baptist's declaration with what the prologue of John's Gospel states: "But to all who did receive him, who believe in his name, he gave the right to become the children of God, who were born, *not of blood, nor of the will of the flesh, nor of the will of man, but of God.*"

He as the Lamb of God became a sacrifice for the children of God, who are the sole ones to see their sin borne or taken away. The Lamb of God by sacrifice was not merely making it possible for sin to be taken away as contingent

Since it lay in the sovereign will of God to save, so that it does not ultimately lie in the will of man, it stands to reason Christ's sacrifice could not in any way be in vain.

on the human will. His sacrifice in itself took sin away, and did so before many became children of God. John Murray observed: "(The sacrifice was accomplished) without any participation or contribution on our part. A work was perfected which antedates any and every recognition or response on the part of those who are its beneficiaries."

What are we to make of the declaration that the Lamb was to bear or take away the sin of *the world*? John in his Gospel is very fond of the word "world", and it assumes several meanings, depending on the context. Even with respect to the world being viewed in terms of people, it is used at times with a tentative suggestion.

When it says Jesus was in the world but the world did not recognize him, it is clearly not referring to everyone actually living at the time when as the Word he became incarnated (1:10). When Jesus' brothers mocked him and said, "Show yourself to the world," they clearly did not have every living being in mind (7:4). And other such instances as found in John can be multiplied.

An important matter to keep in mind about John's Gospel is that it was a gospel written by a Jew for a Jewish audience. For the Evangelist 'the world' in terms of salvation meant that which comprised both Jew and Gentile, since Jesus' plan was the salvation of both Jew and Gentile—"the world" therefore from a Jewish point of view. While we can safely assume that Jesus as the Lamb of God became a definite sacrifice for those born of God and not through the will of man, the primary import behind the Baptist's declaration was simply that Jesus was to suffer vicariously for Jew and Gentile.

Lightfoot goes so far as to ask if it is possible that the Baptist without an audience states Jesus is the Lamb to take away the world's sin when he might well have been reticent so soon to speak of the universality of the Lamb's sacrifice. When he declares again Jesus is to be the Lamb for the world's salvation, he John definitely has an audience of two of his own disciples, who are Jews, beginning to impress upon them the truth of the universality of God's salvation. The tenor of John's Gospel is such that the Baptist's exclamation is no doubt interpreted by the Evangelist to mean that Jesus' sacrifice is for Gentile as well as Jew, though perhaps the exclamation was deliberately directed to a limited audience at a time when it was too premature to suggest too widely and too publicly salvation was for the Gentile as well.

The Evangelist's intention through interpretation of John the Baptist's declaration is clear: Jesus as the Lamb of God would become a sacrifice and throughout his gospel there is much evidence to show that Jesus would not die in vain but that he was destined to carry away, to put away the sins of all who are the particular people for whom he suffered, be they Jew or Gentile.

REDEMPTION IN JOHN

John 3:16: *"For God so loved the world, that He gave His only Son, that whoever believes in Him should not perish but have eternal life."*

Frequently regarded as the epitome of the Gospel or the good news, all the same John 3:16 has often been misunderstood when it comes to applying it in preaching and evangelization.

More than likely, John 3:16–21 is the reflection of John the Evangelist and not that of Christ, since the pericope carries certain expressions not recorded elsewhere of the kind found on the lips of Christ. John 3:16 embraces the essence of Jesus' teaching through the medium of the Evangelist, words unlikely to have been heard from Jesus by Nicodemus, "the teacher of Israel."

The question first arises: If John 3:16 embraces John's reflection, why are these words of God's love for the world inserted at this point in the Gospel? This, after Jesus had finished speaking to Nicodemus, "the teacher of Israel"? It would appear that John is setting out early in his Gospel to emphasize in his somewhat Jewish-orientated work that Jesus came not merely to save Jews only, for *whoever* believes will have eternal life. The word "whoever" is carried over from Jesus' discourse with Nicodemus, and so is found as part of John's own reflections (3:16–21 again). As Westcott observes: "The Evangelist (is led) to unfold (the meaning of Jesus' words) more fully in relation to the actual circumstances in which he was himself placed." That is, John, in composing his Gospel many years later, applied what were Jesus' words to "the teacher of Israel" to that which had become in a later time the obvious fact that Jesus was also the Savior of Gentiles.

The beginning of John 3:16 can be rendered: "Indeed, *in this way* God so loved the world" .... In the way that any Israelite could believe in order to be spared of death, in the way even any Israelite such as Nicodemus could believe for eternal life. In what way would God express his love, or in what way would men discover it? In a way similar to what was required when the people of Israel were commanded to look up at the bronze snake on the pole in the wilderness, and when many of them were dying by snake bites through their disobedience to God (John 3:14,15 with Num.21:9).

Yet, when looking up at the raised Son of Man, in similar manner the Gentile could find eternal life too, should he also look up and place faith in the Son of Man. As is noted later in the Gospel, John shows he had become aware that Jesus had in mind the Gentiles when he spoke of "other sheep" that he has. He came that "he might be revealed to Israel" (1:31), but he later declared that he came to lay down his life for sheep other than those of his own race. Is not this the burden of John's Gospel to a large degree?

At the outset of John's Gospel it is stated: "He came to his own, and his own people (as a nation) did not receive him.*But to all who did receive him* (by intimation 'the whole world') . . . ."

God had clearly loved Israel and chose her above other nations, and his love for the believing individual among those of Israel was most evident. Would it not be most evident also among all Gentiles who acknowledged Jesus as their Messiah that God had a special love for Israel? Note that when Jesus speaks to Nicodemus, it seems there is a particularism in that the Son of Man (an expression uniquely known to Jews through special revelation) speaks through the channel of Nicodemus about the need for people in Israel to be born again. He is concerned for the need of the teacher of Israel to be born anew and in turn, by implication, for Nicodemus to teach others in Israel what he has heard for his hearers' salvation. Yet the particularism is superficial. John's reflections (after 3:15) are not in any way at variance with Jesus' teaching. What John reflects on as a contemplation of Jesus' discourse with Nicodemus is similar to what Jesus himself is to say later concerning Gentiles. John in effect in reflection on Jesus' discourse with Nicodemus is saying: "Does God only love Israel, only gave his Son for Israel? No, God loves the Gentiles too." In that sense God loves the world.

And on the heels of John's reflection about God loving the world and not condemning it, and after showing how the Baptist exalted Christ, the author reflects yet again (vv. 31–36) with some

---

Preachers would do well, when preaching on this great text, to keep in mind the astounding fact that a Jew such as John came to see that God loved *the world*—was there anything of this kind stated before Christ became incarnate?

editorial that timely precedes the story of Jesus meeting the woman of Samaria in such an encounter that finally leads the Samaritans to exclaiming that Jesus is the Savior of the world (4:42).

In conclusion we simply say that "For God so loved the world" ... means his love extends to Jew and Gentile, without it being understood to mean that he has died for every person who has been, is now, and ever will be in the world so as to save them. It is incorrect to read into John's reflection the false assumption that many read into it. It is even a false assumption—though far less damaging—to read into this particular passage that God's only intention is to save the elect by the giving of his Son, as John is only stating God loves Jew and Gentile—that alone was "scandalous" enough even for many a believing Jew.

No individuals here in John 3:16 are identified as objects of such divine love. This means that the task of the preacher and the evangelist, when expounding John 3:16, is merely to herald the news that God loves Gentiles as well as Jews now, and exhort their hearers to believe. Based on what else is stated about salvation, there is no necessity to encourage hearers with "God gave his Son for you." Never in the Early Church in evangelism was it said to any individual: "God gave his Son for you." We are simply to announce the good news about salvation, and those who come under its spell will be those who are born through God (John 1:13). It remains good news in the announcement of it. Nothing is lost by not applying the truth of Christ's sacrifice so "personally" via the preacher, but all is gained when it is the Spirit who stirs the heart to embrace Christ effectually.

> John 4:42: "(The Samaritans) said to the woman, 'It is no longer because of what you said that we believe, for we have heard for ourselves, and we know that this is indeed the Savior of the world'."

John is very fond of the word 'world'. He employs the term 69 times as against the leaner usage of it by the other gospel writers—Mark 5 times, Luke 7, Matthew 10. Of course, it is used in various ways by John, but it is most frequently employed by him in a soteriological sense. John 4:42 finds it referring to Jesus as Savior of the world.

Clearly in this case the term "world" calls for an understanding of John's Jewish perspective. In the story about the harvest being reaped by Jesus among the Samaritans, John notes in his Evangel that the Jews—John's own ethnic people—had no dealings with the Samaritans, therefore when the despised Samaritans believed Jesus to be the Christ, it is apposite for the Samaritans to claim that he is the Savior of the world, that is, a Savior of the Samaritans as well as the Jews.

The Samaritan woman was surprised that Jesus would ask her for a drink, but the element of surprise did not end there. From his conversation with her, it became evident that the Samaritans worshipped God in a different way from that of the Jews, though on the surface the woman was expecting the Messiah to come and "tell us all things." We say "on the surface" because it is likely that the woman spoke of 'the Messiah' in deference to Jesus, for the Samaritans preferred "Taheb" which, according to Carson's commentary, translates as "the Restorer", or possibly "he who returns." From this we may conclude that, strictly speaking, no soteriological significance was found in what the half-breeds in the Samaritans expected in the appearance of "Taheb", whereas right-thinking Jews were expecting more than a prophet, anticipating a king for spiritual reformation- and a Jewish king, one destined to rule in some favor to the Jews but in a benevolent universal sense.

Now, while the woman most likely referred to "the Messiah" in deference to Jesus (v.25), it appears that upon leaving him, and on further reflection, she came under the suspicion that Jesus was not so much "Taheb", and not even merely a Jewish prophet but the Christ, the spiritual King the Jews were expecting. Her posed question back in town is asked with some hesitation: "Can this be the Christ?" Still, it is asked as based on the possibility that Jesus was the Jewish Christ or King. It implies her fellow Samaritans had some understanding about the coming Jewish King. Then, once Jesus had stayed with the Samaritans for two days they were surprised, but convinced he was both Savior and King for them too.

There are other occasions where in the Evangel of John the term "world" has a restricted meaning, as it often does in Western circles today. "World" does not connote universalism as commonly and theologically understood in many evangelical circles when basing it on the likes of the exclamation of the Samaritans—that is, Jesus is the Savior of everyone who has ever lived.

The original language carried no punctuation at all, but J.B. Phillips captured the amazement that ran through the Samaritans by the following—

"We know now that this must be the man who will save the world!"

> John 6:33: *"For the bread of God is he who comes down from heaven and gives life to the world"*

When Jesus discourses on being the Bread of Life after being found again at Capernaum, at least some of those who had been fed by him on the northeastern shore of the lake were there at Capernaum to hear the discussion that followed the miraculous feeding of many across the waters. Presumably the greater part of the crowd was Jewish, as they say to Jesus: "*Our fathers* (emphasis mine) ate the manna in the wilderness" . . .

> The Samaritans were surprised to learn that Jesus is the Savior of both Jew and Gentile, and that he would bend to be their Savior too.

Yet when Jesus speaks of giving something greater than what Moses gave, he calls himself the Bread of God, as not given simply for the Jews but for the world. He is conscious of the growing antagonism of his own people towards him as a whole, and firmly places his hope of giving life to many among the nations who are bound to believe in him, since Jesus was to go on to say that all that the Father will give to him will come to him.

The querulous audience may have been too occupied with Jesus claiming superiority over Moses to have noticed the universal note about the Bread of God. If the Jews had no dealings with Samaritans, for instance, one would think that the Jews would take umbrage at Jesus' universalism, but nothing is said by way of objection. Was Jesus superior to Moses? Unlike the grumblers in his audience, Jesus stayed not with his claim of superiority over Moses, but sought to fix his opponents' minds on what was to be accomplished in giving life for the world. Therefore we find him pressing the point of universalism when he invites the crowd to acknowledge the uniqueness of the bread of God in him: "If anyone eats of this bread, he will live forever. And the bread that I will give for the life of the world is my flesh." Not simply "anyone" among the Jews could live forever, but "anyone" in the world.

Emphasis is thrown throughout the whole Bread of Life discourse on "anyone", "whoever" and "the world." Obviously, there was eternal life offered both to believing Gentile and Jew, though such a truth apparently had not been grasped by the crowd at Capernaum.

In this discourse about the Bread of Life, Jesus makes it clear that it is the Father's will that he will lose nothing of all that the Father gives him. So "anyone" in the world, be he Jew or Gentile, is simply one whom the Father gives to Jesus and who will come to Jesus. The narrow-minded of Israel did not understand these twin truths of both universalism and election, but our Gospel writer did, and consequently prefaced his whole unique testimony of the words and works that Christ did with both the truth that all who are born of God are born not of the will of man but of God with the truth that rang out in John the Baptist's prophetic cry of "Behold, the Lamb of God Who takes away the sin of the world."

Yet, "anyone", "whoever" and "the world" need not imply any person has the natural ability, or even the co-operative ability to believe in Jesus. It simply means anyone, be he Gentile or Jew, will be found among the believing.

"Anyone", "the world" . . . these terms need not imply that there is "an atonement sufficient for all, that all are salvable, though not all are saved, in consequence of his death," as Bishop Ryle suggested. While some admit Christ's death is only profitable to those chosen by God for salvation, they maintain "Christ is for every man", just as Ryle believed. Are the likes of Ryle correct? While Christ's atonement is effectual only for the elect, is it efficient for the non-elect? Ryle's view was a common sentiment shared also by many at the Synod of Dort in 1618–19 in the Netherlands, by those called Contra-Remonstrants, who actually believed that it is only through the prevailing, persuasive will of God that people are saved, and therefore sought to emphasize the prevailing design of God for Christ to die for the elect, but among them at Dort a large number claimed that the death of Christ was sufficient as an atonement for both the elect and non-elect. These Contra-Remonstrants, in opposing the Remonstrants who championed more tolerance of belief in general among the churches of the Netherlands, are said to have desired to solve all issues related to the extent of the atonement on the basis of the Scriptures, though not all of them were out necessarily to appease the Arminians.

In good numbers the Contra-Remonstrants maintained Christ's death was in theory sufficient for the sins of whole mankind, but was it on the basis of the Scriptures?

The Canons of Dort, which were drawn up to summarize the Calvinistic beliefs of the Contra-Remonstrants, actually provided no Scriptural support for the belief stated in Article 3, under the Second Head of Doctrine and titled The Death of Christ, and the Redemption of Men thereby, which reads—

> "The death of the Son of God is the only and most perfect sacrifice and satisfaction for sin, and is of infinite worth and value, *abundantly sufficient to expiate the sins of the whole world* (emphasis mine)."

The Canons of Dort were not exactly replete with Scriptural quotations to buttress the various doctrines the Contra-Remonstrants championed, but that which dealt with The Death of Christ, and the Redemption of Men Thereby has none at all, except in the body of the related Rejection of Errors, which refutes in the main the notion that God had ordained his Son to death "without a certain and definite decree to save any" . . . , and that which also refutes wholesale universalism. In Rejection of Errors some Scripture is quoted in the rebuttal of listed errors but only employed carefully to indicate God had in mind the elect when Christ died, and that classic universalism was not in the design of the atonement. It was not considered an error to believe Christ died only for the elect.

Although it is said that many statements of the groups of delegates from different countries attending the Synod of Dort may be considered too brief or too abstruse to lend themselves to more definite positions of belief, it appears that not all the groups of delegates present consented to Article 3. Those of Emden stated that "Christ died by the intention and will of the Father *only for the elect* (emphasis mine)." Those of Gelderland: "Christ died *vice& loco* the elect only." Those of Overijssel simply defined their position with: "The absolute will and intention of God in delivering His Son to death was to acquire the remission of sins for the elect." Among those of Great Britain there was a difference of opinion over the atonement's extent, with some insisting Christ only paid the price of redemption for the elect, but they felt a compromise was needed in order for the Canons of Dort to come monolithically into effect, therefore they all helped Article 3 to become one of the nine articles pertaining to the doctrine of the death of Christ.

While there are those of us who read into Jesus' words about him being the Bread of God that gives life to all—both the elect and non-elect—through his atoning death, his words need not imply any such thing. Jesus speaks to a Jewish audience—to a unique and singularly blessed people of the past—simply telling them in a broad way that he came to give life to both Jew and Gentile, to give his flesh as life for both Jew and Gentile. This is the simple way Jesus' Jewish hearers would have understood him, if they were spiritually alert.

> John 10:14, 15: *"I am the Good Shepherd. I know my own and my own know me, just as the Father knows me and I know the Father; and I lay down my life for the sheep."*

After the incident concerning the Jewish authorities throwing out the man born blind from the synagogue, it was apposite for Jesus to move on from speaking metaphorically about himself as Light to likening the religious authorities to false shepherds or thieves of his flock, and to speak of himself as the Good Shepherd who has a flock that recognizes his voice, and for whom he is even prepared to lay down his life. The time for Jesus to die was nearing and therefore he makes it clear that his death will be intentional and salvific for his flock.

A careful reading of Jesus' words should make it crystalline that at first Jesus speaks of a large enclosure that contained sheep belonging to several owners, as Carson makes clear in his commentary. Jesus comes as one of the shepherds to bring out his particular sheep from the enclosure. The gatekeeper opens the gate for him. Jesus calls out his sheep from the other sheep. They then follow him.

When it became clear that Jesus' audience did not understand the cryptic figure of speech, he changes his manner of speaking. As Carson notes: Jesus is no longer the shepherd but the gate or gatekeeper, no longer leading a particular flock out from the enclosure as a single event, but leading his own in and out elsewhere. We can add now that Jesus has in mind his sheep's own pen—not that belonging to several owners. The sheep imagery is sustained throughout, but a change in the manner of speaking finds Jesus claiming that he is now the gate of his own flock which has its own enclosure. Yes, at first the emphasis lies on Jesus as the shepherd who calls out from other sheep his own, after which the emphasis (revealed in vv. 7-18) is on Jesus having his own sheep in possession, with a willingness to lay down his life to secure them.

This means that Jesus as the good shepherd lays down his life only for his sheep.

The effect on Jesus' sheep would not be one of uncertainty; it rested on what is known as effectual calling. We are not to press the sheep imagery too much but, if it is not completely convincing in this passage alone, elsewhere John's Gospel makes it transparent that only Jesus' sheep respond to his call, because they are divinely designed to do so willingly (see John 1:13, for instance). There is no hint in Jesus' parable that sheep other than his own heed his voice and follow him so that his willingness to lay down his life in death would be efficacious for elect and non-elect. Only for his sheep does he lay down his life.

> He calls out his sheep from others who do not stand to gain from his death.

THE SCANDAL OF GOD'S FORGIVENESS

> John 11:51, 52: *"(Caiaphas) did not say this of his own accord, but being high priest that year he prophesied that Jesus would die for the nation, and not for the nation only, but also to gather into one the children of God who are scattered abroad."*

Much commotion had arisen because of Jesus raising Lazarus from the dead, and as a consequence many from among the Jews were found through this sign and other ones believing in Jesus. The popularity of Jesus alarmed the religious authorities who feared the destruction of the nation by the Romans, who would more than likely suspect a possible rebellion against them by the Jews. Caiaphas spoke of the public benefit or expediency there would be if Jesus were to be executed.

John informs us that Caiaphas said more than intended. He prophesied ironically that Jesus' death would benefit his own nation as well as "the scattered children of God."

We are to understand by "Jesus would die for the nation" that the nation was the nation of the Jews. We ought not to slip into the notion that "the ultimate 'holy' nation is the church" (*pace* Carson), as the plain and sole meaning here is that Jesus would die on behalf of (*huper*) the Jewish nation simply to avoid any overthrow of the nation by the Romans. In that sense Jesus' death would have no salvific effect.

Caiaphas did not know what he was saying but he was looked upon as having the final word on issues related to the nation, and was often considered as a prophet thereby. Therefore, even stating that Jesus was to die for the nation was considered prophetic, because of the nature of his office as high priest. To the believing Jew it would have been seen as an evil word because to his mind Jesus was the longed-for Messiah, yet unbeknown the political expediency lent itself through its anti-salvific intentions for good. Divine providence took up the base motive and made use of it in order that not only the Jewish fold of believers would gain eternal life because

---

Yet, while dying in a non-salvific manner, his death would become salvific for all the children of God—comprising both believing Jews and believing Gentiles.

of Jesus' death but that the Gentiles would as well. Many Gentiles lived outside Israel, of course, and so did many Jewish believers-to-be. All God's children were scattered, scattered throughout Israel and beyond. Jesus desires to bring them altogether (John 10:16 with 11:52).

We also observe that Jesus was to die effectually for all the children of God. Some endeavor to hang the truth of his death on the contingency of the human will for its effectiveness to save and thus entertain the notion of uncertainty (in theory at least) about the possibility of any person or many people possessing faith that is sufficient to ensure that Christ's death becomes effectual, but doubtless the Johannine accent is on a definite divine plan to not only bring about his death but to ensure his death would prove efficacious for those destined to be God's children. *The plan to beget children of God (John 1:12,13) was just as certain as the divine plan in ensuring that the death of the Savior begot children for God.*

> John 12:32: *"And I, when I am lifted up from the earth, will draw all people to myself."*

Carson makes the pertinent point that arising from the fact there were Greeks who wished to see Jesus, he, in speaking of the kind of death he was to die, had in mind "all people without distinction, Jews and Greeks alike" becoming drawn to him. Carson is careful to establish that Jesus did not contemplate the drawing of all individuals without exception.

While it is true that people of every nation, tribe and language are drawn to him, it is more definitive to think of "all people" simply in terms of Jew and Gentile, since the people of Israel—the original hearers of Jesus' words—were accustomed to view the world in such a way, just as we are emphasizing.

Christ speaks doubtlessly of an effectual drawing, not one that just momentarily attracts and then loses its pulling power. Some in preaching on Jesus' words imply such ineffectual attraction. No, Jesus speaks of the kind of attraction alluded to earlier in the Gospel, where it states: "No one can come to me unless the Father who sent me draws him."

THE SCANDAL OF GOD'S FORGIVENESS

> John 12:37: *"Though He had done many signs before them, they still did not believe in him, so that the word spoken by the prophet Isaiah might be fulfilled . . . "*

While there is no allusion in these words of Jesus to his death and the extent of his atonement, this passage is chosen from what are a considerable number that speak of unbelief in Jesus for the purpose of exploring what exactly constitutes unbelief in relation to him. For it is common for many believers these days to appeal to unbelievers by saying "Jesus died for you." This issue has already been touched on (see under John 3:16) but it needs to be dealt with more fully.

If we hold that Jesus did not die or make atonement for everyone, then what exactly makes for unbelief regarding him? Does it lie in refusing to believe that he died for us personally? If we do not believe in him for salvation, does our unbelief or disbelief have anything to do with rejecting him on the grounds that he died for us? What does John say in his Gospel of this, if anything?

It is safe to say that when Jesus began his ministry, belief in Jesus' name did not embrace the doctrine of the atonement, when such a doctrine was yet to be understood as essential for the actual saving of believers. It was not known nor understood. This we keep in mind when it stated in the beginning of the Gospel that all those who received him and believed on his name were given the right to become children of God. A knowledge of all that could eventually be required to possess eternal life—including the redeeming death of the Lord—was hardly expected to be comprehended in early days. Sufficient it was to welcome him as the Lord and the Giver of eternal life, as the Messiah or King of Israel. We do not even know what exactly the Baptist understood when he announced Jesus as the Lamb of God. John's announcement is quite strange in the light of the Synoptics portraying the Twelve grappling with Jesus' claim that his death was a necessity. All the same, John as the author of the Gospel has much to say about belief and unbelief with regard to salvation, much of which was understood in hindsight after Jesus' resurrection.

John 1:12 circles around the fact that belief in Jesus' name had to do with believing that he was God and was the Word of God, believing he is the light of life. Into a dark world he came; a true believer was conscious of the darkness and was prepared to welcome Jesus as the unique divine Light. And we can say that in the early days on the aforementioned grounds alone, Jesus gave all believers then and there the right to become the children of God. The question of "Do you trust that Jesus is to die for sins?" lay beyond the parameters then.

Even with a post-resurrection understanding of the atonement, the question could ever only be "Do you believe Jesus died for sinners?"

In those early days we do find Jesus talking to Nicodemus about the new birth and linking it with the necessity of his death. He refers to the lifting up of the bronze snake by Moses—likening that lifting up with his own. Did Nicodemus perceive what was meant by the Son of Man being lifted up? It was beyond his comprehension at that time.

Therefore, it was rather inconceivable for Jesus to ask Nicodemus, "Do you believe I am dying for you?" Nicodemus lay in a state of unbelief, and Jesus only cryptically states that he by necessity must be 'lifted up' so that eternal life becomes available to anyone who would place faith in Him. Nicodemus

> "Only when Nicodemus saw Jesus on the cross, or perhaps only still in later reflection on the cross, would it become clear that the 'lifting up'/exaltation of Jesus took place on a brutal block of wood on a forsaken site outside Jerusalem" (Carson)

is to become a believer but it was—as it was always in the Early Church—after a blanket invitation to place faith in him who was to be "lifted up" for unnamed sinners. Jesus was to die for Nicodemus but Nicodemus sensed no conviction about it until he was conscious of sin, alive to the truth Jesus died for sinners, and then arriving at a conviction in terms of a given assurance that Jesus suffered for him. It was not only inconceivable for Jesus to ask Nicodemus "Do you believe I am dying for you?" because it was "early days" for any to understand about the means of redemption, but because it was not the question to ask the teacher of Israel when it was not personally revealed if Jesus was personally dying for Nicodemus or not. The promise of eternal life is always bound up with what we may say is the mere knowledge Jesus was lifted up for all who will look up in faith to him, any who will look up to faith to him. There is a general invitation to believe, but it is another matter to learn if Jesus died for anyone of us in particular.

As for unbelief, it follows that it was condemned even before it became clear that atonement by Jesus' blood was required for salvation. Unbelievers in early days were condemned because they did not believe "in the name of the Son of God" (John 3:18). John tells us that people were declared guilty because they "loved darker rather than the light because their deeds are evil" (John 3:19). Exposure by Jesus of people's evil deeds was sufficient in itself to condemn them. The same is true today, even though atonement by Jesus' blood is common knowledge. For even when the atonement was seen post-resurrection as being the essence of the Gospel, the Scriptures never urged missioners to appeal to unbelievers to place faith in Christ on the grounds he died for them personally. Unbelievers are not directly or instantly bound to believe Christ died for them.

How does an unbeliever arrive at the truth or the conviction that Christ died for them? How are they effectually drawn to it? Let Turretin, a famed Reformed scholar of the sixteenth century, explain.

Turretin in his brilliant work of *The Atonement of Christ* shows that a person must believe *mediately* (to use Turretin's term) before he or she *immediately* and convincingly believes Christ died for them. Faith and repentance are the mediate acts necessary for salvation. Turretin says that the object of evangelizing is to have the unsaved aware of the promises of the Gospel, promises firstly pertaining to the word of God, and secondly to the need to acknowledge through repentance and the exercise of faith that Christ is "the only sufficient Savior." (We may add that in tune with John 3:18, this matter of promises is what gives the Son of God his trustworthy name). According to the Reformed scholar the first two *acts* required by the unsaved, upon becoming conscious of the promises of God are: Assenting to the word of God, and then "laying hold of Christ" by faith. Only then can the third act take place: That of believing Christ died for *me*.

So it is that "Christ is not revealed in the Gospel as having died for me in particular; but only having died in general for those who believe and repent."

Thomas Goodwin, who had a commanding influence on the well-known Westminster Assembly in the seventeenth century and was of Independent persuasion, in his *Object and Acts of Justifying Faith* shows that God gives eternal life "with the most serious purposes and unchangeable resolutions" to we humans, but he does not tell you "the names of persons who are numbered among the saved." This he is saying with respect to the issue of the Gospel invitation. Although Goodwin sets out in his work to demonstrate the promises pertaining to eternal life are general and has in mind more the subject of election, and not that of the extent of the atonement, his point is quite identical to Turretin's: The invitation to eternal life is a general one to all, and only proves personal among those to whom God intends to give eternal life.

Turrentin introduces a syllogism:

(A) "I know Christ died for all who fly to Him"

(B) "I find that I have fled to Him"

(C) "Hence I can and should infer that He died for me"

Therefore we see that unbelief is condemned on grounds short of the charge that one rejects to their condemnation that Christ died for them. And it can be demonstrated that no one knows if Christ died for him or her personally until they exercise faith and repentance as required of those who seek eternal life in him. Even when "restricted" by witnessing the signs Jesus wrought, and not possessing a knowledge of the Messiah's intention to die for a salvific purpose, Jesus' hearers were condemned for their unbelief so that they could not be "healed" of their hard hearts (12:40).

John 15:13, 14: *"Greater love has no one than this, that someone lays down his life for his friends"*

Jesus addresses his disciples with parting words before he goes to his crucifixion. He seeks to comfort them with the assurance that they are his friends.

While it may be claimed that it is not explicitly stated that he is prepared to lay down his life only for his friends and no one else, Jesus' words of assurance suggest that he is not unaware of those who are the objects for salvation through his atoning death, thinking that he could die in vain, that he would die perhaps fruitlessly for other than his friends. That he was destined to die only for those who were certain to be his friends appears to be the natural meaning of his words.

Some cite Romans 5 to show Jesus died for his enemies. One commentator—McDonald in his *Believer's Bible Commentary*—even goes so far as to say that Jesus' disciples were Jesus' enemies when he died for them, yet Jesus had already pronounced them "clean" when he washed their feet before he died, and before death he likened himself to a vine of which they were a part. It is true that he died for all whose sins had alienated them from being friends—including those of his chosen disciples of the time—but we ought not to cloud the issue: The disciples were already friends when he spoke of laying down his life for them. It is safe to say that he also was prepared to lay down his life even for those who in advance would become his friends.

The friendship between Jesus and his immediate disciples was conditional to a degree upon their abiding loyalty to him (as John makes plain), but his preparedness to lay down his life for them points to a friendship that was unconditional. As Carson says: "(Their) obedience does not make them friends; it is what characterizes his friends."

With regard to Jesus' assurance of his friendship for them, another thing of interest lies in what he further says to his disciples in order to comfort them. On the heels of speaking of them as friends he says that they did not choose him but he chose them and appointed them to bear fruit. Yes, they were chosen to serve but not

---

Election is linked with particular redemption. It is no accident that many of those, who take the doctrine of election seriously, believe that Christ solely died with the elect in mind. Few, who believe in election and God's sovereign and prevailing grace, will hold that Christ died for all people, once or if they are exposed to the teaching of particular redemption.

only for that: They were chosen for salvation, as a careful reading makes plain.

In quite a well-balanced work of *Hand in Hand* Alcorn confesses that he holds to the doctrine of God's sovereign and prevailing grace for salvation, but claims that he has difficulty accepting the belief that Christ died only for the elect. He appeals to seven texts that "seemed" to substantiate that Christ died for all people when he first became convinced of sovereign grace, which "still seem" to teach the same thing for him after many years. He contends that "many Calvinists" hold a similar belief to his. It can be said "many" do not. If a so-called many do, it may well be that they have been subject to an Arminian past, and even though they have come to hold at last the true doctrine of God's sovereign grace in salvation, for them it appears that a belief in a more universal atonement is not irreconcilable with the truth of sovereign grace in salvation. They have not examined the matter exhaustively, or perhaps have never been exposed to the possible view that only the elect were those for whom the Lord suffered.

For if God has elected some for salvation so that his love for them is unconditional, and it is not merely contingent on foreseen faith, then it is natural to assume that Christ died only for the elect. He was not destined to die in vain, or with any degree of uncertainty as to its efficacy. He was to lay down his life for his friends because he chose them not merely for service but for salvation. The hatred of the world was to be levelled at Jesus' own because he chose them out of the world (v.19). They were to be objects of hatred as Jesus was.

As it has been already alluded to under "John 6:33," many of those representatives and advisors at the Synod of Dort in the Netherlands in the sixteenth century, in seeking to establish what became known as Calvinism throughout the land, in addition to affirming a certain doctrine of limited atonement, contended as well that the suffering of Christ is sufficient for the atonement of the sins of all men, but for us there is room for elaboration on this point.

There were those at Dort that held that Christ died for the elect, and spoke only of Christ dying for the elect, without reference to any suffering for the redemption of all people, but the majority—one after another—declared that Christ's death was sufficient in itself to expiate the sins of all mankind, though the death of Christ was effectively paid for the elect (as previously discussed). Of course, it was possible for Christ through his death to establish a sufficient atonement for all, but did he? Was such a point of dogma merely a sop that most in attendance at the Synod of Dort provided in order to mollify their Arminian opponents in the Remonstrants?

In elaboration on this point, we may well ask: Where was the Scripture to support such a notion? It may appear more jarring to hold that Christ died only for the elect- with no benefit at all for the rest of mankind- than to believe that God chose and intends only to save certain people, but it is actually no more jarring.

Again we say that there is a sense in which there is logic behind what is known as classic universalism. For if it is asserted that Christ's death was sufficient enough for the redemption of all men, it stands to reason all men will be saved. While it may be claimed in opposition to classical universalism that people must exercise faith to make Christ's death effectual, if it is true that Christ became a most worthy substitute to make atonement, then by the very nature of substitution all are saved.

> It stands to reason that if God out of his unconditional love intends to save some and not others, then Christ's death only occurred salvifically for the sake of those who are the objects of that unconditional love. This John 15 bears out with both its emphasis on Christ laying his life down for his friends, and on his friends merely comprising those chosen out of the world to know the Father (vv.15–27).

No Scripture lends support for believing that Christ's suffering was a sufficient atonement for all, while he died only effectually for the elect. Such a belief smacked of evangelical scholasticism at the Synod of Dort. Such a hypothetical notion sought to make "unlimited atonement" a pleasing point with the Remonstrants in view—all without Scriptural warrant.

Whence did the notion arise that Christ had died sufficiently but not effectually for all? No doubt it was influenced to a degree by Scripture that speaks of a certain universality to do with his suffering. For instance, we read "God so loved the world that he gave his only Son" . . . .Yet, let us reiterate: John's Gospel is Jewish, and when "the world" is spoken of in relation to redemption, his Gospel is to be viewed through Jewish eyes, seeing the world as "us and them", observing that Jesus had come surprisingly to save Gentiles too. There is a deafening silence about sufficiency without efficacy: Jesus was definitely destined to die for his friends, those chosen out of the world to be so. In this way it is an "unlimited atonement": He died for all those who are destined to be friends. They are the sole reason why he died.

Redemption in Acts

> Acts 16:6: "*And (Paul, Silas and Timothy) went through the region of Phyrgia and Galatia, having been forbidden by the Holy Spirit to speak the word in Asia*"

PAUL, WITH HIS CO-WORKERS in the Gospel, was on his second missionary journey. Without going into the complexity of what constituted the regions of Phyrgia and Galatia—whether Luke had in mind ethnic territories or the Roman provincial divisions of that area—it appears Paul was travelling westwards and intending to pass on to the Roman province of Asia where Ephesus was situated. The Holy Spirit blocked his path, therefore he decided to travel north to Bithynia, passing the edge of Asia. Yet the Spirit (called the Spirit of Jesus this time) forbade him to go north as well.

We may not know exactly the whole reason for the Holy Spirit forbidding Paul and Silas to preach the gospel in Asia, and also the reason why the Spirit of Jesus forbade them to go north of where they were, yet the restraining power of the Spirit has a bearing on the doctrine of the extent of Christ's atonement, as we shall see.

Only a small number of commentators have ever sought the reason for the restraint being imposed on Paul and Silas. David Brown of the nineteenth century suggested that firstly, in all probability, Europe and not Asia was "ripe for the labors of our (sic) missionary party." Then he suggested that "other missioners (like Peter) were to have the honor of establishing the Gospel in the eastern regions" of what Brown termed as Asia Minor, meaning Bithynia among other places of the north. Brown based this on 1 Peter 1, where we read "Peter, an apostle of Jesus Christ, to those who are elect exiles of the dispersion in Pontus, Galatia, Cappadocia, Asia, and *Bithynia* (emphasis mine) . . . "

With respect to the divine forbidding of Paul and Silas to travel north to Bithynia, it would seem that Peter eventually went to Bithynia, but only at a considerably later time than when Paul travelled through Mysia. Moreover, Peter was a missioner to the Jews while Paul was set apart for the Gentiles, therefore it is questionable if Peter would have covered the area of Bithynia extensively so as to evangelize among the Gentiles in that region also, when he went with the Gospel.

With regard to the restraint of the Holy Spirit on Paul and Silas to head into Asia, it is conjectural—Brown employing the word "probably"—to claim Europe was a more fertile area than Asia for the Gospel. Only the Holy Spirit knew if it were more fertile, because it is not exactly stated as to why the two were blocked in the path to Asia.

It all comes to this: Even if Europe would later prove to be more fruitful for Peter than at the time that Paul and Silas were passing through, and even if Peter was to arrive later to evangelize Bithynia more comprehensively than we imagine (when he is actually reckoned to be a missioner to Jews only), there were bound to be people who would not hear the Gospel at all on account of the restraint of the Holy Spirit on Paul and Silas at that time. There would be people in Asia and Bithynia who would not hear the Gospel to their salvation between the time Paul did not pass through and Peter passed through. Some perhaps in those places may have heard to their salvation later on, but it requires little imagination to be convinced that many never heard the Gospel, just when Paul and Silas came short of where those people resided. If this is so, then can it be said that Christ died for all mankind, or even that his atonement was sufficient for all?

In answering objections to the belief that Christ died only for the elect, Turretin, in his comprehensive work *The Atonement of Christ*, responds to the opinion that maintains "redemption was procured for all with a design that it should be applied to all, provided they would not reject it." Turretin says that such an objection loses its force when one observes that there are an innumerable number of people to whom Christ has never been offered, and who do not know him, even in name. The opinion that the Reformer counters has Christ dying for those to whom he never reveals himself.

Many are unreached for salvation—not only because missioners fail to reach them but because the Holy Spirit, the Spirit of Jesus, designs it to be so.

> Surely Christ could foresee through the centuries that there would be people who would never hear the Gospel. How can it be said he died for them? Christ was not to die for those who could not possibly believe.

Try as many missions do to reach great numbers among the nations, even in our time there is bound to be innumerable people who will never hear.

This should never dampen the desire to evangelize. In fact, it has not. Many of the foremost pioneers in overseas missions in the nineteenth century believed in what has become known as "particular redemption." Indeed, belief in such a doctrine inspired them to preach the gospel throughout the world, as they knew that the Spirit of Jesus, while blocking the way in one or more directions, was to lead them to where there would be those who proved responsive, just as Paul and Silas received a vision to head for Macedonia, where the likes of Lydia would have their hearts opened by the Lord to pay attention to the good news (Acts 16:14).

> Acts 17:2–4: "And Paul went in, as was his custom, and on three Sabbath days he reasoned with them from the Scriptures, explaining and proving it was necessary for Christ to suffer and to rise from the dead, saying, 'This Jesus, whom I proclaim to you, is the Christ'. And some of them were persuaded and joined Paul and Silas, as did a great many of the devout Greeks and not a few of the leading women"

Although it has already been stated under the comments earlier on in "Luke 22:19–23" that we never read of the Early Church proclaiming in their evangelism to anyone that "Christ died for you," in addition to some observations made in the Lukan passage, there is a need to probe even more into the way the Gospel was presented in early days in terms of Christ's death.

For a typical example, we find Paul explaining and proving to those in the synagogue at Thessalonica that Jesus is the Christ. We do not know in detail how he explained Jesus is the Christ—though Acts 13 provides some kind of guide as to what he may have said at Thessalonica. The gist of what he said was that Jesus is the Christ.

While Luke omits detail, there appears to have been no personal application or invitation of "Christ died for you" made to Paul's audience at Thessalonia—merely it "was necessary for Christ to suffer." As to the exact beneficiaries of his atonement, nothing was proclaimed by Paul to the effect "Christ died for you."

When Paul spoke over three Sabbaths to his Thessalonian audience, he did not know who might have been the beneficiaries of Christ's death, the objects of his grace. He did not know until he saw some signs to indicate Christ had died effectually for any in the audience. Not until some were "persuaded" and "joined" Paul and Silas did it become it clear as for who Christ died among the listeners.

> If personal application had been as paramount as it often is in many evangelical circles today, it would have naturally emerged in any situation similar to that in the synagogue of the Greek city with the personal appeal being taken up in evangelizing and in the appeal for people to repent. Yet, as elsewhere in Acts, it is not stated by Paul or anyone else that "Christ died for you."

We read that some Thessalonians were persuaded. They were not persuaded at least at first that Christ died for them personally. Then, how did they know that he did? Luke does not tell us at this point but he does not need to, as earlier in Acts he relates how one needs to have faith in Jesus' name (Acts 3:16). One can see how persuasion works so that faith then is exercised, and the persuasion is of God. Believers are such because they have been appointed to eternal life (13:48), that it is the Lord who opens the door of faith through his grace, that he opens hearts of people to pay attention to the Gospel and believe (16:14).

Therefore, nothing can prevent those who will truly believe from believing. In evangelism the first thing to declare in respect to the atonement is that it was necessary for Christ to suffer. This is tantamount to declaring God is not reluctant to save sinners. The gospel invitation is accompanied by God's promises to save sinners. The call is to believe the promises, even if they at first appear indefinite, or in a sense "impersonal"—the evangelist and the hearers at first do not know who among the hearers will prove to be among the saved. Still, the call is to believe, and God's promises will prove to be definite and able to be personally applied if the hearers believe Christ died for sinners, such as they are. All are invited to believe, for without qualification God's promised word stands. Do we believe? If we do in order to be justified and cleared of our guilt, then we have been persuaded, and this by the secret work of the Holy Spirit.

Redemption in Romans

> Romans 3:23: "... *for all have sinned and fall short of the glory of God.*"

IT IS NOT UNCOMMON to think that by *all* Paul is saying such a thing as there is "no difference between drunkard down in the gutter and the man of morality (outside of Christ)", but what he does mean exactly when he refers to *all*?

While the apostle's statement does not directly touch on the extent of Christ's atonement, the exact subject of the pronoun shows up how many of us out of evangelical habit can easily misconstrue the import of *all*. While it may be true that there is no difference between a drunk and a secular moralist—since both are sinners—this is not what Paul exactly had in mind when he penned ... "for all have sinned" ...

We can too easily lose sight of the Jewish perspective and the drift of Paul's argument in Romans at this point of 3:23. Many have been sensitive to the distinction between Jew and Gentile in Paul's mind when considering what he writes earlier on about the differing states of sin Paul outlines in Romans, but they "forget themselves" by misconstruction as to what is meant by *all* when arriving at the exegesis of 3:23. Even able scholars such as F.F. Bruce have lost sight here of the Jewish perspective. He writes of "the participation of all in 'man's first obedience' "—claiming the context suggests this—"but here (in 3:23) we have here rather a statement of the fact that all men, as *individuals* (emphasis mine), have sinned." Yet, is Paul, by employing *all*, stressing men's individuality as sinners?

Lloyd-Jones spent 13 years expounding Romans and, in a detailed exposition of 3:23, speaks of "the Law (that) no longer applies," therefore "no longer must anyone think of saving himself." By referring to the Law it is presumed that Lloyd-Jones has the written

Law in mind. This approach may be seen as reading back into the apostle's words an eisegesis based on modern man's thinking. We of our modern civilization may well be acquainted with the Mosaic Decalogue—thanks to Christian influence—but Paul only spoke of *the Jews* failing to keep 'the Law', not the Gentiles. He writes in Romans of the Gentiles "sinning without the law." The Law of Moses was only given to Israel. As for the Gentiles, "by nature they did what the Law required, even though they did not have the Law." John Murray in dealing with the complex matter of Romans 2:14f. claims that the Gentiles did not exactly follow the Law but did "the things of the Law," such as "the pursuit of lawful vocations, the procreation of offspring, filial and natural affection, the care of the poor and the sick." Through the knowledge and practice of some things they also betrayed their unwillingness to obey God internally, when they suppressed what was plain to them about God (Romans 1:19f.).

As Paul saw it, the Gentiles did not and could not contemplate any attempt to obey the written Law that was uniquely given to Israel.

When Paul writes earlier in 3:19-20 that the Law—embracing the whole of the Old Testament—led to the world being accountable to God, he means that while the Law spoke to those under the Law, that is, the Jews, every man as typified by the Jews is stopped so that *the whole world* becomes accountable to God. For while the Gentiles did not possess the written Law as the Jews did, yet they were not without excuse, just as Paul had already demonstrated in Romans 1; if they had had the privileges of the Jews they would have gone the way the Jews did.

It may be correct to state all men fell into disobedience through Adam's sin, that every individual has sinned, that people of all classes and types have sinned in any given society, but Paul's thrust had to do with highlighting the lack of distinction between Jew and Gentile, especially when the Jew was tempted to

---

We can say that in the light of all that Paul wrote previously in his letter, things were brought to a grand conclusion in 3:22b-23. Once he established in detail that Gentile and Jew alike had sinned in their peculiar way, he stated there was no distinction between Jew and Gentile—both Jew and Gentile had sinned and come short of the glory of God.

view himself as superior because of his acquaintance with the written Law.

Therefore, we contemporaries ought to be cautious whenever we meet the word *all*, not merely in Romans but elsewhere in the New Testament. Much is achieved by seeing through the Jewish eyes of one such as Paul in order to discern accurately the original intent behind what was written in the Scriptures.

A sound exposition of Romans 3:23 will attempt to highlight the fact that both Jews and Gentiles are sinners, that the written Law proved to be of no soteriological advantage, but that in the absence of the written Law the Gentiles were without excuse. It is pivotal to consider the little difference there was between anyone who only knew of God in nature and a work of a law in their hearts, and anyone who had clearer light through the Law written out. "For *all* (Jews and Gentiles) have sinned . . . ."

> Romans 5:18: *"Therefore, as one trespass led to condemnation for all men, so one act of righteousness leads to justification and life for all men."*

When Paul continued on in his letter to the Roman believers, could it be that when we encounter the word *all* once again, that Paul as a Jewish believer still remains conscious of the former distinction that was drawn between Jew and Gentile when thinking of sin, or does that distinction collapse when thinking of justification and sanctification? Could it be that in his Jewish way of viewing the Gospel, he continues to employ *all* in terms of a Jewish and Gentile contrast when it came to considering "death in Adam, life in Christ"?

While it is evident that death spread to every individual in the world and that one trespass led to the condemnation of every one irrespective of whether or not they were Jew or Gentile, it is possible that it is not exactly what Paul meant by *all* when applied to the spread of death and corruption. It is feasible that *all* sustains its initial import even in Romans 5. The apostle's words could be paraphrased to signify that death spread to Gentile and Jew, meaning that one trespass led to the condemnation of both Gentile and Jew. That his Jewish consciousness is still present when dealing with the issue of death in Adam and life in Christ is evident in his reference to death reigning from Adam to *Moses*. A paraphrase to embrace the apostle's Jewish consciousness could well lend also to a consistency that proceeds to *all* in Romans 5:12–20.

It would lend to a consistency to counter the claim of classical universalism, which can appear logical (theo-logical) if it is contended that Paul is saying all who have ever lived are condemned by one trespass, and therefore one act of righteousness leads to life for all people so that everybody who has ever lived will be saved. This so-called logic is inspired by Paul's statement in v. 18—

> "Therefore, as one trespass led to condemnation for all men, so one act of righteousness leads to justification and life for all men."

As it is, evangelicals have traditionally been quick to define the second "all men" so that it assumes another definition from that of the first "all men," evangelicals qualifying the second one by the terms the apostle himself employs in "many" and "who *receive* (emphasis mine) the abundance of grace . . . .", thereby it is evident that not all people are recipients of justifying grace. This form of reasoning is sound, and yet it overlooks Paul's 'Gentile-Jew consciousness'.

Some may say, "Is it of any consequence to overlook this Gentile-Jew consciousness?" Yes, it is. It is needful to recall Paul's initial depiction of the state both Jew and Gentile were in—one state with a kind of law known in the conscience and through nature, and the other with more enlightenment through the Mosaic Law. While sin came into the world through one trespass, many trespasses grew from the one trespass under two distinct circumstances. The marvel was that grace came to those less privileged through not having the Mosaic Law, and that it even came to those who sinned in the face of their knowledge of the

---

Paul's "Gentile-Jew consciousness" sounds out a greater depth of understanding the grace of God in Christ. It also contributes to countering classic universalism by defining even more closely what Paul understood by "all men." Both Jew and Gentile had been overpowered by death. Both Jew and Gentile were condemned. Both Jew and Gentile are recipients of the free gift of grace. By "all men" Paul has in mind in the main Jew and Gentile.

Law of Moses. Grace came to those who did not even live by the dim light given (and who were defiant in the dim light given, as the Old Testament repeatedly reveals), and it came to those who possessed the brightest of light.

Even Paul's Gentile readers would have felt that degree of the apostle's Jewish consciousness since he makes it clear at the outset of the letter that the Gospel is to go to the Jew first, and that glory and honor and peace first belong to the Jew (1:16 with 2:10). We do well to keep in mind how originally the letter came to be, the circumstances that led to it being written, the thinking of its author and his readers of the time (Pawson's chapter on Romans in *Israel in the New Testament* is elucidating on this score).

> Romans 14:9: *"For to this end Christ died and lived again, that he might be Lord both of the dead and living."*

That Christ did not die in vain is evident in hindsight because many people have been saved through his shed blood down the centuries, but in foresight was it apparent that his death was certain to bear fruit? The question is considered in the light of a large passage that is just as neglected as Romans 9–11—we speak of Romans 14–15. David Pawson is quite correct in claiming that Paul is not saying through Romans "This is my Gospel," but that the apostle is insisting "This is the Gospel that unites you (Jew and Gentile) and makes you one." After outlining in Romans that both Jew and Gentile have sinned and therefore are on level ground, Paul shows how both can be saved by grace through the redeeming work of Christ. In his bid to warn the believing Gentile of a lapse into antinomianism and the Jew of a lapse into legalism, Paul then strives to achieve a unity among Jew and Gentile in the Roman congregation. He touches on Christ's objective in dying, as it relates to unity in the church.

Note also how sizeable a portion Romans 9–11 is in the apostle's letter. He seeks to demonstrate that God has not forsaken the Jews as the Gentile believers of Rome might well have believed. It was crucial for the unity in the Gospel for the Gentiles to acknowledge God's love for Israel despite her large scale rejection of Christ. Those who do not acknowledge a further restoration of Israel in

God's plan of salvation often pass by Romans 9–11. Yet, it is not a parenthesis, and it is not essentially written for Jewish believers. It was written for Gentiles who were tempted to think God was finished with the Jews, which temptation threatened to break up the unity in the Roman church.

Therefore, we are not to be surprised if Romans 14–15 in particular has to do with Paul's effort in quite a practical way to unite, or keep united, the believing Jews and Gentiles. The whole purpose of Romans obviously lies to a considerable degree in the attempt to unite the Roman church. Much of the earlier part of Romans is taken up with the issues of sin and the need for salvation because both believing Jew and Gentile were meant to see that the Gospel with its implications already united them. The Gospel makes them one, so both were potentially able to worship together.

It is the worshipping together that explains Romans 14–15, with Paul first outlining the disputable issues that threaten to break up the unity and may invite divine judgement (14:1–6) before he raises the matter of the reason for Christ's death and resurrection. Unfortunately, believing Jews and Gentiles often worship separately even in our day—frequently being unable to adapt themselves to one another over questions to do with feasts, Sabbath observance and Kosher food—and it says much favorably for the Roman church of Paul's day, when Jew and Gentile saw the potential to worship as one. Paul presumes that what he says will be realized and lived out in his readers. Irrespective of whether or not they abstain from certain things of indifference, they all do not live for themselves, neither die for themselves. If they live, it is to the Lord. If they die, it is to the Lord. Whether they live or die, they are the Lord's. This is why they were not to judge one another. Then at this juncture the apostle speaks of the object of Christ's death and resurrection.

Christ died and lived again for the purpose of possessing us as His own. Regarding this, he did not die in vain. He died so that we would live and die as his. "For this end Christ died and lived again," says the apostle. Fact: each believer lives out his life and prepares to die as in Christ's foresight and foreordination. Christ's intended aim in death could not be frustrated. *He alone secured the ability of the believer to live and die as unto Him.*

Strictly speaking, the extent of Christ's atonement is not in view in Romans 14:9, but Paul's words infer Christ did not die in vain, could not die in vain. There is no direct word about him dying for the elect only, yet the design of his death is there under view. He did not die in the mere hope that some would put their trust in him, nor did he die in doubt that the believer would fall away and be no longer his. Yes, he died for those ordained to be his own (see earlier the apostle's words in Romans 8 and 9).

With express purpose and determination, and through his death and resurrection, Christ had in view his lordship over the living and the dead among believers, and thereby secured in death and resurrection his lordship. As Lord then, he was certain to accomplish it. No one by nature seeks after God (Romans 3:11), but God has mercy on whomsoever he wills (9:18). We are the Lord's, no matter whether we live or die, because in both his death and resurrection he already had us in mind in order to save and preserve us. In death we are helpless, in life no less helpless without him being Lord.

> Romans 14:15: *"By what you eat, do not destroy the one for whom Christ died"*

These words logically follow on the heels of those in 14:9f.—still dealing with the same matter of being careful not to offend our weaker brother over a matter of indifference. Yet, it raises a question concerning the efficacy of Christ's death: If it is maintained that Christ did not die in vain because through foresight and foreordination he undoubtedly purchased those who were to believe, how can it be that a believer may be "destroyed" if Christ died for him or her?

A weaker brother may become grief-stricken if he is coaxed into a so-called liberty that violates his tender conscience. It is in this sense that it is said that he is "destroyed." It is not stating that the weaker brother will no longer be saved in the end. If it spoke of eternal condemnation for the weaker brother, it would stand to reason that the stronger brother would suffer similarly, since he shares by his action in the cause of the destruction of the weaker one. As it is, the stronger brother is merely cautioned against causing a weaker brother to stumble, though the doubting of the weaker one is "condemned" if he eats not in faith. The condemnation is not defined as eternal.

Also, it is to be observed once more that no unbelieving individual is ever said to be "one for whom Christ died", as it is expressed concerning the weaker brother in Rom.14:15. Throughout the New Testament it is both frequently and only stated that Christ died for those known to be saved, those who are "called", those of 'the church'. It is natural that it is stated Christ died for the saved when letters such as Romans were addressed to the saved, but we never read that on the occasions when the unsaved were called on to repent for salvation that the appeal hinged on Christ having died for them, though it became evident that he had died for some to whom the appeal was made, once any of them in Early Church days were persuaded to place faith in him.

To some it may seem that Christ died for the weaker brother in vain, as the stronger one is warned of the danger of destroying "the one for whom Christ died." Yet, if it be that "to this end (of becoming Lord of all the believing, whether they be dead or alive) Christ died and lived again" (recall v.9), Christ cannot lose one of his own to eternal destruction. The weaker brother may be made to stumble and be destroyed in that sense, but Christ's intent in his death cannot be frustrated.

Redemption in 2 Corinthians

> 2 Corinthians 5:14: "For the love of Christ controls us, because we have concluded this: that one has died for all, therefore all have died; and he died for all, that those who live may no longer live for themselves but for him who for their sake died and was raised."

WHO ARE THE "ALL" for whom Christ died? To appreciate Paul's divinely-inspired words we should observe the drift of the apostle's thinking.

The drift of Paul's word is frequently overlooked when considering the above text, with the text itself on close examination correcting what is commonly accepted as proof of a universal atonement.

To begin with, in this Corinthian epistle the apostle has *believers* in mind as he writes of reconciliation. He states we all—apostle, Timothy, and all believers—must appear before the judgement seat of Christ "to receive what is due for what he has done in the body, whether good or evil" (vv.9, 10). Then the apostle proceeds to say: "Therefore, knowing the fear of the Lord, we persuade others" (v.11). Although these words of v.11 are commonly applied for evangelistic purposes, the truth is that these words have believers in mind. The apostle is stating that because *believers* must fact the judgement seat of Christ, he and Timothy were constrained to persuade believers to fear the Lord in the face of the coming judgment. What Paul and Timothy are is known to God, but Paul confesses that he *hopes* that what is known about Timothy and himself in relation to God is known to the Corinthians as well. Are they aware of Paul's status as an apostle of God, aware of his deep sincerity and love for them?

Paul is appealing to the believing Corinthians all the way. The ESV translates "I hope" (v.12), which may suggest the modern connotations of "hope." *"Hope may be well-founded in probability or completely impossible" (A Modern Guide to Synonyms).* Philip Hughes is quite correct in holding that a common meaning for *elpizo* is "believe", thus he says of Paul: . . . "he believes that in (the Corinthians') heart of hearts they know that he is sincere and genuine." Paul adopts the word *elpizo* because up to the time of writing *the Corinthians are yet to be convinced that Paul is genuine and sincere*. Paul is genuine and sincere and he is straining to persuade the Corinthians that he is authoritative, except that the strain is there even though Paul has the belief and confidence that they will learn eventually that Paul can be trusted as a genuine apostle. It is a hope based on a probability, based on a past indication of a kind, the past indication being that the Corinthians are believers, therefore they are people to whom Paul can make an appeal with confidence. Paul truly hopes, and believes and hopes with no misguided confidence.

The love of Christ was controlling Paul and Timothy ("us") so as to appeal to the Corinthians to come to their senses and realise that Paul is a genuine apostle. And the appeal would not be futile, as Christ died and rose again in such a way that caused the believers of Corinth to die and rise so that they "might no longer live for themselves but him w*ho for their sake died and was raised"* (v.15).

Paul has opponents who are pseudo-apostles and who are jostling for the Corinthians' attention (v.12). If he is "crazy," then it is for the Corinthian believers' sake (v.13). The apostle is driven by the fact that the Corinthians are the objects of Christ's love, Christ having died and rose again, in a death and a resurrection of a kind that they also entered into. They the Corinthian believers died and rose again when Christ did. Christ loved them to certain salvation even when he died and rose again.

Not a few scholars have introduced Adam into the drift of Paul's appeal to those of Corinth, but any reference to the sin of Adam and its universal effect of death for all is not strictly relevant. The apostle does not refer to Adam. The subject at hand is the believers' death to sin and the consequent participation in the fruit of Christ's death through his resurrection.

Despite efforts also to utilize Paul's words to support classic universalism, the apostle actually has in mind "the limited intention of Christ's death" (Arthur Pink). Christ is said to have died on behalf of the believers at Corinth (and in fact all believers, needless to say), for it is said "He died for all," meaning he became a substitute. As a substitute, he "discharged the obligation of those for whom it was rendered"(A.A.Hodge). As a substitute he satisfied God's requirements of us—... "he died for all, therefore all have died." Moreover, as Turretin says: ... "it cannot be said that he died for any others than those for whom he rose, because no one will be a partaker of the fruit of Christ's death, unless by his resurrection."

Paul knows with confidence the Corinthians believers can be appealed to in two ways: (A) His appeal is no empty one, as it is the love of Christ himself that makes the appeal through Paul and Timothy, (B) Christ himself is appealing to those who have already died to sin through the efficacy of his death, and who through his resurrection are bound to live "for him who for their sake died and was raised."

One cannot avoid passing over the voluminous *The Sovereignty of Grace* by Arthur Cunstance who claimed, while espousing the doctrine of what (we repeat) is not too wisely descried as "limited atonement", that the text under question suggests an inclusiveness that actually goes beyond what is traditionally understood by many as "limited atonement."

> We can see Paul is solely occupied with the welfare of actual believers. Universalism is far from what he had in mind.

Custance argues that our text "may indeed be interpreted to signify a certain *universalistic* aspect (emphasis mine) of the Lord's death." Not unlike a few other scholars, he drags the issue of Adam's sin and the consequent universal death for all men into the arena. (He incidentally errs in holding that the referents of the 'us' in the text are the Corinthian believers, whereas we are insisting that the "us" is Paul and Timothy, making their appeal to those in Corinth). By bringing the issue of Adam into the arena, Custance attempts to distinguish 'sin' from 'sins'. For him 'sin' relates to man's sinful condition, while 'sins' belong to man's sinful actions. Sins are what we are aware of. Sin has to do with what we are unaware of. Sin closely connects us with Adam, what we are unaware of. When it comes to the Judgment, Custance suggests that it would not be just for God to condemn us for the condition of sin and what we are unaware of. He proceeds to say Christ died for sin and sins. Since he died for sin and what we are not aware of, and that such sin is common to all mankind, Christ died for everyone. As a consequence, all men will be liberated from being a mere mortal creature; "all men will be equally raised from the dead, *freed forever* from this present physical defect, and will therefore face judgment in bodies no longer subject to death."

It is strange that Custance seeks to buttress his thesis with the words of John 5:25 and 29, which words spell out nothing less than a coming condemnation for all those who have done evil. To go beyond the power of physical death and be resurrected in order to know only eternal condemnation can hardly be viewed as that which Christ died for, can hardly be viewed as a ransoming of *"all men's bodies from the grave."* In the labyrinth of Custance's thinking, he is unconvincingly attempting to persuade us that Christ died for sin as well as sins, and that therefore unbelievers can be reckoned as ransomed because all men are implicated in what they are not aware of. He does not argue too openly for the case of classic universalism but one wonders if classic universalism is coming in the back door, even though Custance speaks of some deserved condemnation for unbelievers.

It is a certain concept of underserving condemnation that spectre-like ought to trouble the reader of Custance, since he claims "all men equally will be raised from the dead, *freed forever* (emphasis mine again) from this present physical defect (through possessing mortal bodies), and will therefore face judgment in bodies no longer subject to death." Freed forever? It can hardly be

---

Christ died for the sinful condition of believers, as well as for the sins of which we are conscious. There is no warrant to hold that Paul in 2 Corinthians is saying Christ died for the sinful condition, and since all people at least have that sinful condition, Christ died for all people.

termed "freed forever" if it is a resurrection to eternal condemnation as Scripture sees it.

The distinction between sin and sins, though drawn to a degree in the Old Testament sacrificial system, just as Custance observes, is false at this point.

The apostle does not distinguish between sins and sin, and when he speaks of Christ dying for "all", he has in mind all those who have died to sin with all of its effects in Christ and who have the divinely-given potential to "no longer live for themselves but him who *for their sake* died and was raised."

What was the King's intention when he died? Recall that "Christ" stands for "King." As King he died, sovereignly planned to succeed, for those who would no longer live for themselves. His intention was clear. It was not to be frustrated. As the King, could he die in vain? So, as King, he exercises his prerogative and therefore Paul proceeds and confidently presses for the Corinthian believers to be reconciled to God.

It is quite common to regard Paul's appeal for reconciliation as an evangelistic appeal to unbelievers (vv.16–21), but he and Timothy ("we") do not have unbelievers in mind at all, even though he refers to God reconciling the world to himself. Firstly, he says that he and Timothy regard no one in the flesh, not Christ, not the Corinthians, when once they even had judged Christ on a superficial appearance. They now saw him as "Christ", "King"—the Anointed One appointed to save his people from sin and eventually rule over the world. Since having come to their spiritual senses, Paul and Timothy regard all believers as new creatures, embracing the Corinthian believers who as Gentiles formed a large part of the church at Corinth. Paul as a Jew speaks of God reconciling the world, for he knew as a Jew that God was reconciling Gentiles to himself as well. This reconciliation saw Paul, a Jew, through the ministry given to him and Timothy ("us"), beseeching

> The very nature of redemption through the death of Christ requires us to acknowledge that his death was purely designed to save only those who have been chosen out of the mass of mankind for adoption as sons of God.

the Corinthians to be reconciled to God, though the Corinthians were believers.

Paul needs to remind the believers at Corinth why Christ died: He was made sin who knew no sin, so that in him they may become the righteousness of God.

Paul is concerned that the Corinthians, though not unbelievers, are not taking the chances to do what is good, to come to their senses about Paul's status, to become more discerning while they were alive in this world. Paul had a more embracing and wider view of salvation in the present life for believers than many of us have. It was up to the Corinthians to open their hearts to Paul and Timothy, as they had opened theirs to them.

> Although as believers they had become new creatures in Christ, Paul and Timothy appeals to them "not to receive the grace of God in vain" (6.1) in order to become more fully the righteousness of God. All this was on the basis that every one of us must all face the judgement seat of Christ.

Christ died for all those who have died—died to sin. Not having died *in sin* but died *to* sin. And those who have died to sin now no more live for themselves. Quite clearly, as Paul presses on to urge the Corinthians to be reconciled to God, he knows with confidence that he can appeal to them because God is appealing to them through him, and because they are new creatures in Christ. He is begging them not to live for themselves—not out of anxiety, as they have died to sin since Christ became sin for them.

Those at Corinth (like all believers) have died when the old has passed away and the new has come (v.17), and they are not to live for themselves but be reconciled to God. This is what undergirds Paul's word about how and why Christ died when he speaks of all for whom Christ died.

Redemption in Ephesians

> Ephesians 1: 1–14: *"Blessed be the God and Father of our Lord Jesus Christ who has blessed us in Christ with every spiritual blessing in the heavenly places, even as he chose us in him before the foundation of the world, that we should be holy and blameless before him. In love he predestined us for adoption through Jesus Christ, according to the purpose of his will, to the praise of his glorious grace, with which He has blessed us in the Beloved. In him we have redemption through his blood, the forgiveness of our trespasses, according to the riches of his grace, which he lavished upon us, in all wisdom and insight making known to us the mystery of his will, according to his purpose, which he set forth in Christ, as a plan for the fullness of time, to unite all things in him, things in heaven and things on the earth.*

GEORGE HERBERT, THE GREAT English poet wrote a poem called *The Water-course*, in which some critics see ambiguity in the final lines—

> "Who gives to man as he sees fit {Salvation (or) Damnation."

Does God give salvation to some because God in his sovereign will sees it fit to do so, or does he give salvation to some because they have made themselves fit enough to receive it? In short, is salvation contingent on the human will or the divine will? In Herbert's case one critic rescues us from the dilemma by pointing out that Herbert, being an Anglican clergyman, doubtlessly subscribed in his time to the Thirty-nine Articles of the Church of England with its doctrine of salvation as an unearnt blessing, and as dependent solely on divine determination. The critic must have also been of this persuasion concerning Herbert because there are quite a number of other poems by Herbert cited to confirm the critic's viewpoint.

Even if there appeared to be any ambiguity in *The Watercourse*, no ambiguity ought to exist about the fact of election for salvation in Ephesians 1 being according to God's sovereign will alone.

The only alternative explanation to believing that election is solely due to God's sovereignty for certain people is perhaps the one that the writer has encountered from time to time—the belief that the whole of mankind has been chosen, the claim that all have been chosen but that many do not choose to be chosen!

Yet, election in the mind of Paul stands for some being *picked out, taken out for oneself* (ek-leg-om-ahee). God has picked out, selected from the mass of mankind some out of his personal interest and their advantage for salvation. The original word implies that he chose wisely and carefully what served his highest interest. Being holy, God has a high interest in holiness, but also he chose and predestined some out of love and the desire to adopt them to be sons in fellowship with his Son, who also is loved of him. From an unholy and blameworthy world God has taken for himself the predestined people for a salvation that Paul insists is one that is dependent on God's will and pleasure entirely. Those who are chosen are not elected because they are "holy and blameless"; they have been chosen before the foundation of the world and they become holy and blameless as a result. Paul speaks only of his readers and their kind—not the whole of mankind.

Modern translations have broken up Ephesians 1:1–14 into a number of sentences for contemporary readers, but Paul's opening words to those of Ephesus form one sentence, a sentence of 202 words. Paul not only pours forth phrase upon phrase, and praise upon praise, when contemplating the prospect of God's eternal purpose in bringing his sovereignty into full reality by uniting all things in heaven and on earth under the headship of Christ, but in that extended sentence he is embracing three things of significance that are pertinent to the point of this work of *The 'Scandal' of God's Forgiveness*–

A. God has exercised his sovereignty and pleasure in choosing some for salvation.

B. God has exercised his sovereignty and pleasure in redeeming the predestined through Christ's death.

C. God has exercised his sovereignty and pleasure in choosing among the predestined many Gentiles as well as Jews.

Enough has been outlined concerning the selection of some for salvation out of God's predestined purpose—as I disclosed it from vv.3-6—but, since Paul links the redemption made possible by Christ through his extension of praise of salvation for believers, it is natural to see the intent behind *the death* of Christ in the light of predestination.

What is the nature of that redemption? Paul is saying that in love God predestined believers through Jesus Christ, who provided redemption through his blood. The word *apolootrosis* stemmed from a word to signify the purchase of a slave at the slave market. As a word *lootrosis* was strengthened by a preposition in front of the noun to signify the unparalleled purchase Christ made when he "purchased (us) from the slave market of sin" (see Strong's Exhaustive Concordance). Picture a slave: helpless, in a state of bondage, a captive deprived of liberty, his will playing no part in his predicament so as to improve his lot. He cannot gain freedom unless someone sets him free. He cannot be set free unless someone purchases him. With respect of believers, Christ paid the price.

There can creep into the picture of the purchase for the slave that notion of the desire of the slave to be free so that the efficacy of the ransom is contingent on the desire of the slave to be freed. Yet, it is not torturing the text to bring into the image of the slave in the slave market the truth that in the case of a believer, he has been predestined for freedom. For Paul clearly links grammatically and theologically predestination with redemption by Christ's blood. It is an actual redemption predestined that sets a man at liberty.

Also, *apolootrosis* has the connotation of a ransom, as well as that of a slave (Bauer, Arndt, Gingrich). "What is a ransom if not setting a man at liberty?" (Calvin). It is predestination that determined it to be so. A ransom is a payment to deliver one who is in a state of powerlessness and is being held as a captive, liable to lose his life unless a ransom is paid for deliverance.

From this we can deduce that Christ died only for the predestined, who alone will be purchased, ransomed or redeemed by God's eternal purpose. Christ died for the forgiveness of sins, it being the outcome of the shedding of his blood, with a forgiveness that is bound up with the prerogative or the pleasure God has because of his sovereignty. If one is forgiven, it is because he or she was predetermined to be forgiven. If one is not forgiven, it is because he or she was not predetermined to be so, though one should more than hesitate to speak of "double predestination" as some do, for the non-predestinated are still responsible for their sins, just as prisoners who are not released according to the Governor's Pleasure remain in prison on account of breaking the law of the land.

As predestination is grounded in the divine prerogative, so too is forgiveness of sin. God is free, not bound to forgive all of mankind. A pardon implies the authority to waive punishment, and implies the authority to withhold it, without being unjust. This is "the scandal" of God's forgiveness. And forgiveness is in this sense no more a "scandal" than predestination, or that Christ died for the elect. If God predetermined some for salvation, forgiveness of the chosen was foreseen and foreordained. And if Christ's death was foreordained, then his blood was not wasted, nor did his death hang on the contingency of the human will, which human will actually found all mankind powerless to effect their own ransom or release from captivity, or liberty in the slave market of sin.

Lastly, divine prerogative played its part in the calling of Gentile as well as Jews.

We note that Paul does not bother to define close enough the first person plural or the second person plural in verse 12. We moderns may be slow to "catch on" quickly about Paul's use of "you" and "we" as they appear in vv.11–14, for many of us in our day have lost the ability to appreciate the original need for the Gentiles of the Early Church to be

---

Bound up with what is expressed in the linkage of 202 words of praise for predestination, and 'the pleasing pleasure' of God, is the consciousness of Paul in seeing the need to assure Gentile believers that they are inheritors of salvation too.

assured that they were inheritors of salvation as well. Israel was an elect people—and among them there were those who were "the first to hope in Christ (the King of Israel)"—and Paul must go to some length in Ephesians to convince the believing Gentiles that they would be of "the commonwealth of Israel" and inheritors of the promises of God (see Ephesians 2:11–13). This needs to be kept in view whenever it is said of Christ that he died for the world. As we keep saying, it does not have to do with him dying for all mankind, but for Gentile as well as Jew.

Therefore, for Paul it is among the Gentiles as well as the Jews that the elect of God are the objects of his eternal love and the subject of Christ's power to redeem.

Note also that this whole subject matter appears first in a letter that is most pivotal concerning the universal church of God, reminding us that the twin doctrines of definite election and definite atonement are not to be seen as secondary in the doctrine of the church.

> Ephesians 5:25 . . . *"Christ loved the church and gave himself for her . . . "*

Paul lays great emphasis on the church being a body of believers, as he exhorts the Ephesians to strive for unity among each other. The body is one, the body is to grow, and the body is to remain joined and held together by every joint, the body is to be clothed with the new self, the body is to be built up with what is good to nourish it. Then, after ceasing briefly to use the analogy of the body (5:1–21), Paul returns to the imagery concerning the body when he calls on wives to submit to their husbands, since the husband is head of the wife, just as Christ is head of the church. Husbands in turn are to love their wives, just as Christ loved the church. Christ is the head of the church since she is his body. As she is his body, he loves her. Everyone loves his or her own body, cherishing it and nourishing it. Christ cherishes and nourishes the church.

It would be hard to find such affinity as that which Paul reveals here between Christ and his church. In all reverence one can say the word "between" collapses in adequate meaning when the oneness and the union of Christ and his bride is considered—"this mystery is profound" (v.32).

Could not Christ had shown such winning love for those outside the church? Was it just for the church he gave himself so dearly? Was it likely that he would give himself up for anybody in vain and at great cost to himself? Did he not know who exactly was in mind before he gave himself? Turretin insists that in Christ's love for the church there is expressed in his love for his spouse "such a love (that) necessarily excludes a similar love for others." The argument may be regarded as built on an inference only, since here in Ephesians 5 it is not stated that he did not give himself up for those outside the church, but the analogy drawn from the concept of a man choosing one woman to the exclusion of others is difficult to ignore, particularly when the apostle, in telling husbands to love their wives, "does not enjoin husbands to let their love be confined only to their wives" (Turretin). The Italian Reformer expresses how indignation would arise if an adulteress defended herself by exclaiming that Paul did not say to love only your wives.

> Yes, and before he even died, Christ loved the church. Doubtless, his love was antecedent to giving himself up for only her.

Christ gave himself up for the church only, as a man gives himself to his wife only. A man will leave his parents to do this. He will hold fast to his wife. Christ "left behind" those who are outside the church to cling to the church. He loves the church as he loves himself. Before a man gives himself to a woman, he already has had her in mind. Then, once deserting all others, he gives himself only to her.

Redemption in Timothy

> 1 Timothy 2:1–7: *"First of all, then, I urge that supplications, prayers, intercessions, and thanksgiving be made for all people; for kings and all who are in high positions, that we may live a peaceful and quiet life, godly and dignified in every way. This is good, and it is pleasing in the sight of God our Savior, who desires all people to be saved and to come to a knowledge of the truth. For there is one God, and there is one mediator between God and man, the man Christ Jesus who gave himself as a ransom for all, which is the testimony given at the right time. For this I was appointed as a preacher and an apostle (I am telling the truth, I am not lying), a teacher of the Gentiles in faith and truth."*

AFTER ESTABLISHING THAT TIMOTHY needs to "wage the good warfare, holding faith and a good conscience" in the light of Paul exposing the dangers of a shipwrecked faith through not aligning oneself with "the glorious gospel," Paul urges Timothy to have himself and others pray so that a peaceful, quiet life under a sufficiently stable government may aid the gospel going everywhere.

For those who hold to the doctrine that Christ died only for the elect, the words of Paul to Timothy may seem to bristle with difficulty: Is it true that God desires everyone to be saved? Did Christ pay a ransom for everybody? Or, does the "all" in "all people" need to be qualified? And why did Paul then resort to such an asseveration when speaking of being a preacher, an apostle and teacher to the Gentiles on the heels of an apparent universalism to do with the offer of the gospel?

Firstly, Timothy is exhorted to make supplications, prayers, intercessions and thanksgivings for "all people." Actually, the original says: "for all *men*" (emphasis mine). Newbury, who made an

75

interlinear literal translation of this passage, rendered it as "all men." So too did J.B. Phillips, who in translation, by employing a colon, went on to understand "all men" to be "kings and rulers in positions of responsibility." It makes sense to view Paul as having men in positions of authority the objects of prayers and thanks, for males were commonly those in authority in those times. Paul then is employing a form of Hebrew parallelism so that "all people (men)" becomes synonymous with "kings and all who are in high positions." This translation of "all men" would make that which unfortunately has often been changed into a general term for "all people" in translation; fall in more accurately with the reason for praying and desiring "a peaceful, quiet life." After all, not "all people," as it may be generally understood, are of such influence in the way that the ancients saw it—that they can bring about a quiet and peaceful life on behalf of others in society.

While translations such as the ESV render Paul's words to convey the concept of prayer being made for all people in the sense of all mankind (men and women), in addition to and seemingly distinguishing prayer being made for kings and all who are in high places, caution needs to be exercised when one is confronted by *anthropos* (as the original has it), since it has a wide meaning, depending on what the context requires. The NIV translates *anthropos* to mean "everyone", but then with the aid of a hyphen clearly and credibly interprets "everyone" to stand for "kings and all those in authority." This is a sound approach since the "everyone" is only those with enough authority to bring in the required peace and quiet the apostle has in mind. In a politically and sensitive age it may seem impolitic to render *anthropos* as 'adult male,' but it would not have been out of place to do so, since (as it has already been expressed) the apostle lived in an age when those in authority were far more often than not adult males.

How does this relate to the question "Does God desire that all mankind be saved?" Some equate "all people" in connection with prayers and thanksgiving with the "all people" whom God desires to save (v.4), based on the understanding that the same Greek word of *anthropos*—used in association with the subject of prayer earlier on—must convey the same meaning when it comes to the reference to God's desire to save everyone. In both cases it is believed by some that *anthropos* stands for people irrespective of gender. As a consequence it has been claimed that by employing such a link between vv. 1–2 and v.3 that "More would be converted if we (all) prayed more." If one agrees to such a link theologically, the same caution that has to be exercised with regard to the use of *anthropos* in v.1 must be exercised in v.4.

Undoubtedly, *anthropos* can stand generically for people irrespective of gender, but the theological issue of salvation being contingent on prayer needs to be examined.

Still, if salvation is of God, how does it square up with the frequent claim that he desires all people to be saved? Can his desire be frustrated, even if it does not hinge on intercessory prayer for the unsaved? Does the "all people" need to be even further qualified than merely leaving it to mean simply everyone the world over?

> Does the salvation of people depend on our prayers for all? God indeed may make use of means to save people, and such may include prayer, but they are not lost because they are not prayed for. Salvation is of God.

In what particular way may "all people" be restricted in Paul's word to Timothy concerning God's desire and the question of salvation? We should note the train of the apostle's thought. When prayers are answered for a peaceful and quiet life so that believers may be godly and dignified (v.2), then the way opens up to the gospel concerning one God and one Mediator being heard clearly, with people being free of untroubled minds through stable government. So God may well use means for the purpose of salvation—in this case we refer to the means of stable government.

Yet note this: People are to learn of the one God. This is a hint as to who are the "all people." Israel had revealed to the world the one God. Israel were a unique people, and Paul, being a Jew, was unique. So too was Timothy, whose mother was Jewish. The gospel concerns the one God, the God of Israel. The Gentiles served many gods. In preaching the gospel Paul was preaching about a Deity unknown to the Gentiles—one God, which meant by necessity one mediator, the man King Jesus, the Davidic King promised of old to Israel. Consequently, it is in essence a very Jewish gospel.

Being a very Jewish gospel, and with Paul having a very deep-seated conviction that he had been divinely appointed to take that gospel to the unbelieving Gentiles who worshipped many gods, it is little wonder that he roused the ire of his compatriots—even believing ones to a disturbing degree. This explains the reason for Paul writing strongly: "For this I was appointed a preacher and an apostle (I am telling the truth, I am not lying), a teacher of Gentiles in faith and truth."

Thus Paul's asseveration throws light on defining who are the subjects of "all people" when he writes of God desiring all people to be saved. By "all people" he simply has in mind Gentiles as well as Jews. Arthur Pink came closer to the restricted meaning of "all people" than he realized when he wrote that "all" stands for "without distinction of nationalities, social prestige, moral character, age or sex." If in this passage Pink has left his definition standing at "without distinction of nationalities," and further fine-tuned it even more to point out the dissolving of any distinction between Jews and Gentile, then he would have been more correct, as based on Paul solemnly declaring that he had been appointed to go to the Gentiles. For God desires that Gentiles as well as Jews be saved. Young Timothy may have well been intimidated by the Jews so that his confidence was somewhat eroded in being associated with Paul, who, unlike Timothy, had complete confidence that God had appointed him to take the gospel to the Gentiles. Subsequently Paul is declaring to Timothy: "I am not lying, I am telling the truth."

It is of great interest to note that in Paul's letter to the Romans there is a similar asseveration to the one we find in 1 Timothy—when, in writing to the Romans about the greatness of Christ that has made believers more than conquerors, he finds his heart breaking when he reflects on his ethnic people rejecting by and large all the blessings enumerated in Romans 8. Paul exclaims: "I am speaking the truth in Christ—I am not lying; my conscience bears me witness in the Holy Spirit—that I have great sorrow and unceasing anguish in my heart. For I could wish that I myself were accursed

> Timothy needed to be assured that Paul had been definitely and divinely appointed to go to the Gentiles with the Gospel.

and cut off from Christ for the sake of my brothers" . . . As F.F. Bruce observed: "(Paul) gloried in his ministry as an apostle to the Gentiles . . . . But his own kith and kin, the Jewish nation, for the most part failed to accept the salvation proclaimed in the gospel . . . "When there was a tendency in what became a Gentile-dominant church in Rome for the Gentiles to think of the Jewish believers as "poor relations" (F.F. Bruce)—and we add that Paul evangelized most of all among Gentiles—Paul affirms strongly that he still has a heart, a heavy heart, for the salvation of his own race. Thus we see that in the rare case of only two such identical asseverations, they both have to do with the issue of the gospel in relation to the Jew and Gentile question.

The collapse of "all people" into a term that only embraces merely the concept of Jew and Gentile does not plead the case for the divine election of individuals—not even for election itself—but it helps cut the ground from under the feet of those of us who either espouse classic universalism or the belief in any so-called sovereign human will to resist the purpose of God to save whom he wills. God desires to save, but Paul is merely stating Gentile as well as Jew are the ones whom he desires to save. And save he will where he desires—Paul had that confidence, as his letter to the Romans clearly discloses (See Romans 9).

> 1 Timothy 4:10: *"For to this end we toil and strive, because we have our hope set on the living God, who is the Savior of all people, especially of those who believe."*

Because godliness is beneficial in every way, it holds promise for the present life and also for the life to come. We are to be confident that in our struggle to pursue godliness God will prove to be our hope, as he is the living God, the Savior of all people, especially of those who believe.

If we are among those who believe, we receive great heart to observe the way God preserves all people throughout the world, as well as learning of his saving power in we who believe, and who alone know his saving power for eternal salvation.

In what way is God a savior of all people? Is he in any way a savior of all unbelievers in the same way he is a savior of all believers? Do Paul's words entertain the possibility that Christ died for all but especially the elect? There are scholars of Paul's letter to Timothy who assert that God is the Savior of all people in the sense that he made provision for the eternal salvation of all, while he is the Savior of those who have "availed themselves of his provision." Thus the distinction is drawn between God being a potential Savior for all mankind but an actual Savior for believers. The distinction has been described in terms of sufficiency in one case and in the other of efficiency. Yet, such reasoning presupposes that Paul is speaking only of eternal salvation when he writes of God being a Savior for both classes of people.

While not denying that salvation through Christ's death becomes effectual upon exercising faith, it does not entirely or chiefly rest on belief. Paul could write to Timothy about enduring everything for the sake of the elect (2 Timothy 2:10). Because the apostle knew God has his elect to save, the apostle was prepared to endure much in making known the gospel. He shows that the elect "obtain salvation that is in Christ Jesus with eternal glory." Ours is to believe in order to be saved, but one is chiefly saved because he or she is elect.

Nothing was ever said apostolically that Christ's death was sufficient for all in the world, therefore it is safe to say that God is the Savior of all people in a sense that is unlike the way he is Savior of believers. Hendriksen convincingly demonstrates how the term "savior" was used frequently in Old Testament times to speak of physical rescue or preservation, and correctly says that "especially of those who believe" signifies that the term 'savior' has a twofold application.

> In the light of God having his elect and therefore saving them for "eternal glory" (as Paul declares), it is reasonable to conclude that God is the Savior of the rest of mankind in another sense that is not related to eternal salvation.

If God is even potentially a Savior of every person in the world in terms of eternal salvation, then logically it can leave the door slightly ajar for classical universalism in whatever form that may take. Yet Paul does not state that God is a potential Savior eternally of all, but an actual eternal Savior of the chosen. Unless we hold to classical universalism so that we believe all people are eventually and eternally saved, then "Savior" has to be taken in another sense, such as Turretin warns against when he, in line with Hendriksen's thinking, argues that Christ in reality died only for the elect and that God is the Savior of all in preserving and upholding all mankind in this present age. The term "Savior" in a soteriological sense applies just to believers since God is not a Savior eternally of those who will finally perish. Says Turretin: . . . "for we do not call a man a savior who *intends* to save another, but him who does it actually." God is Savior of all—including the believing—with respect to preservation in the present life, but of the believing alone for eternal life.

God saves the believing with "both a bodily and spiritual salvation," and therefore he is Savior *especially* of those who believe. As Fairbairn observes: Paul argues from the lesser to the greater; if God does so much for the unbelieving, how much more will he do for those who believe!

Redemption in Titus

> Titus 2:11–14 *"For the grace of God has appeared, bringing salvation to all people, training us to renounce ungodliness and worldly passions, and to live self-controlled, upright and godly lives in the present age, waiting for our blessed hope, the appearing of the glory of our great God and Savior Jesus Christ, who gave himself for us to redeem us from all lawlessness and to purify for himself a people for his own possession who are zealous for good works."*

IT IS ALWAYS COMMENDABLE when scholars of some caliber take into account the extensive context of a passage of Scripture, and it is commendable that Hendriksen and Fausset have done just that. Both the aforementioned men refer to the instruction Paul gave Titus prior to the wonderful definition of what God in his grace set out to do. Paul had previously instructed Titus (2:1–10) to counsel believers who were male or female, old or young, or slaves, to live consecrated lives so that Hendriksen and Fausset concluded "all people" stands for the grace of God appearing to "men of *all* (Hendriksen's emphasis) these various groups and classes." Hendriksen goes on to equate "all men" of verse 11 with "us" in verse 12. Fausset, together with Custance, stresses the inclusion of the previously-mentioned slaves (v.9) in the "all men" as older translations have it—"all men" defined as all human beings, irrespective of gender, as *anthropos* often requires.

It is somewhat tantamount to saying "God brings salvation even to the lowly people, such as slaves—yes, to all men."

Yet, is this the whole drift of Paul's teaching when he moves on from specific instruction for various classes of believers? I suggest the *gar* at the beginning of v. 11 introduces us to a definition of God's grace that can well embrace the thought of divine grace being for believers irrespective of such classes as had been enumerated earlier by the apostle, but it actually embraces the division among mankind of the kind that Paul as a Jew had in mind.

There is good reason to believe that if Paul's words to Titus concerning the salvation of God coming to all people are similar to his words addressed to Timothy (as 1 Timothy 2 has them), then the apostle had in mind by "all people"—whether latently or patently—the distinction between Jew and Gentile, with believing Jews in the early stages of the church having been compelled to see that God was bringing salvation not only to them but to Gentiles as well. If we refer back to the exposition of 1 Timothy 2:1-7, we note a striking similarity to what we see here in Titus—God viewed as Savior, desiring "all people" to be saved, bringing salvation to "all"—except that the allusion to the Jewish consciousness of the apostle is more obvious in the epistle to Timothy.

> It is to be reiterated that being a Jew, the apostle would naturally and consistently think of all mankind in terms of Jew and Gentile, as based on the ancient revelation of God and the way it was perceived by those of Israel, by those early believers in Christ and who belonged to that definite chosen race.

Common ground in the church today can be established upon agreeing that Paul understood by "all" merely Jew and Gentile, without necessarily applying this with respect to the more specific beneficiaries of the ransom or redemption that Paul regards as the salvific means to purchase a people "for Christ's own possession" (v.14). So much for that common ground showing promise, but in church history we have lost common ground largely over who exactly form the subjects of redemption and this becomes the sorest point among believers. The specific beneficiaries are seen by one school of thought as actually identified at the beginning of the letter to Titus, where the apostle defines his apostleship as being "for the sake of God's elect." The most unfortunate division has arisen down the centuries in the church—not so much between those who define "all" to signify "Jew and Gentile" and those on the other hand who hold that "all" signifies "every living being"—but between those who contend "all" denotes "every living being" and those who claim it represents just "the elect" when "all" calls for the closest definition possible.

Apart from the rationality behind the belief that Christ was not a redeemer through intention but actually, and thereby his death alone was sufficient to redeem, some consideration must be given to the faith that is exercised in the light of election. For it is put forward by not a few that we are elect only if we have first appropriated the benefit of redemption through faith. Faith undoubtedly is a necessity, and "we are actually elect only if we have appropriated the benefit of redemption through faith!" However, for Jew and Gentile, is it grace that prevails or faith? For Paul election is antecedent to faith. Stern, for instance, is in a sense correct in saying that . . . "not everyone is saved because not everyone has committed himself to that grace," but if we ask why they have not committed themselves to this grace, it is not enough to say they do not have faith, since it is only the elect—those chosen out of the mass of mankind—who are destined to have faith, thus Paul was an apostle "for the sake of the *faith* of God's elect."

So God saves Gentiles as well as Jews, but it is the elect of both races who are destined to be saved, the elect being the sole subjects of the redemption Paul spells out as "salvation-bringing grace," which grace alone highlights the dignity of Christ, who is described by Paul as "our great God and Savior." That he should effectually save and redeem those on whom he set his mind before he died befits the honor of his person. It would be beneath the dignity and majesty of Christ to go to his costly death with no certainty that any would become his possession. Even if one person failed to be redeemed despite Christ's intention, Christ would be less majestic than he is—no, he went to his death in dignity to redeem all who were to be redeemed and become his own.

It is grace that prevails. This is why Paul tells Titus that God's grace has shone in that it is "a salvation-bringing grace." To quote Turretin once more: . . . "for we do not call a man a savior who *intends* to save another, but him who does it actually." To this we add: God is Savior, not man, since man is in too helpless a state to save himself.

Redemption in Hebrews

> Hebrews 2:9: *"But we see him who for a little while was made lower than the angels, namely Jesus, crowned with glory and honor because of the suffering of death, so that by the grace of God he might taste for everyone"*

WITHERINGTON 111 SAYS THE author of Hebrews wants to stress that Jesus died "for everyone", "not just for some elect group." He approvingly quotes Chrysostom who said that while Christ died for all, all have not believed even though "he has fulfilled his own part." Yet does the author of Hebrews advance the notion that Christ has come "half-way" and it is left to sinners to come of our own volition for the rest of the way?

It is said by the Hebrews writer that Christ tasted death for "everyone", and does it mean nobody universally will taste death to their ruination? Or, is it that "everyone" does not mean "everyone" in the sense that it is commonly understood? Even if we understand by the tasting of death that it is more than Christ's redemption being available to all mankind on the proviso that it is limited to those who exercise faith and thus gain the benefit of it, we may mean then that the tasting of death by Christ only made deliverance from death vaguely possible, even uncertain so that there might have been no guarantee that any in reality would have come to faith if it hinged on the contingency of the human will. Those of the Open Theism school propound the notion that God can be surprised by human decisions since he does not have the complete certainty of what people may do—there could have been uncertainty as to whether or not anyone would experience deliverance from death, even though provision was made for it through Christ being willing to suffer death for such a deliverance from death for many. Yet, supposing that there was to be people bound to exercise saving faith, what are we to understand by what is said about Christ actually tasting death—"eating" death (Strong), coming to know death (Arndt and Gingrich) for "everyone"? Such a costly death surely was bound to produce fruit for the salvation of some sinners, but for "everyone" as it is commonly understood?

Owen challenged a Thomas More, who was a lay theologian of East Anglia in Owen's day, and who had gained quite a following in support of the doctrine of the universality of the extent of the atonement as based in part on these very words of Hebrews 2:9. Owen marshalled a number of points that must be considered if we wish to arrive at the true meaning behind Christ tasting death for "everyone."

We may politely dismiss one of Owen's points because he claims that by "everyone" the writer of Hebrews has in mind Gentiles as well as Jews. While it was very standard for a Jewish believer in the Early Church to think in terms of Jews and Gentiles forming the ethnic composition of the world, thus frequently employing the likes of "all" and "everyone" with a Jewish consciousness, Hebrews as a letter was written for Jews and therefore by "everyone" it is quite safe to hold that the writer means no more than "Jews." While he has more than Jews in mind when he writes about the future subjection of the world (vv.5–8), and afterwards contemplates Jesus crowned with glory as a forerunner for the future subjection of all, the Hebrews writer definitely portrays the work of Christ for "the offspring of Abraham" (v.16). While it is true also that the work of Christ applies to Gentiles, our writer is addressing fellow Jews who were in need of assurance about the genuine humanity of Jesus, which humanity was in the form of the flesh and blood of Israel's race.

We dismiss that one point Owen makes when he claims "everyone" embraces Jew and Gentile, but consider valid that he is correct in interpreting "everyone" to mean those who become "sons of glory", those whom Christ "sanctifies", those who are "the children God had given (Christ)", who are delivered from the bondage of death, just the Hebrews writer makes clear in the words on the heels of . . . "he might taste for everyone"

On this score, by any teasing out from Owen's observation, we should note that if "everyone" (as "everyone" is frequently understood to be) has had death tasted for them, then why has God only made children for himself from those to whom Christ has been given? For it is written: "Behold, I and the children God has given me."

Also, if "everyone" has had death tasted for them, why will so many not be delivered from the bondage of death? Christ, in tasting death, was tasting and eating it in order that many would no longer be in the bondage of death. Freedom from death cannon help but hinge on Christ having "ate" death.

As Owen in *Death of Death* moves forward when he looks beyond v.9, that is, in exposition to illustrate how "everyone" only embraces all believers in Christ, so we as readers can also move backwards to define accurately "everyone"—viewing what precedes v. 9 to consider "the world to come" (v.5). In the world to come man will have everything in subjection to him and will be crowned with glory and honor, and by "man" the author of Hebrews does not understand it to represent all mankind. Those crowned with glory and honor (v.7) must be the ones defined as "sons of glory" (v.10), and who are said to be brought to glory (v.10). These are they who are no longer under the bondage of death that would otherwise prevent them from seeing the world becoming subject to them under Christ.

So the words of Hebrews work against any notion that Christ died for all universally. He tasted death only for those given to him by God. If Jesus tasted and "ate" death for all universally, then all mankind is no longer under the bondage of death and all will have the world subject to them as sons of glory. Of course, those who believe will physically die, but they shall know eternal redemption when Christ appears a second time "to save those who are eagerly waiting for him" (9:28). As for the unbelieving, there is "a fearful expectation of judgment, and a fury of fire that will consume adversaries" (10:27). We are to understand that by Christ tasting death for the believing, he died not to save them from physical death but the kind of death that will usher the unbelieving into a fearful judgement, to suffer a fury of fire.

Pace Chrysostom, Christ "has fulfilled His own part" and ours as well, if we are numbered among the sons of glory. God has given us to Christ and therefore we respond in faith to believe that he did what we could not do: deliver us from the bondage of death and from the fear of what lies beyond it in judgment if we do not have saving faith in Christ.

> Hebrews 9:15: *"Therefore he is the mediator of a new covenant, so that those who are called may receive the promised eternal inheritance, since a death has occurred that redeems them from the transgressions committed under the first covenant."*

A free translation but more in line with the sequence of the words in the original language would be—

> *"And therefore he is the mediator of a new covenant so that death, having taken place for the redemption of the transgressions under the first covenant, might mean that those who have been called will receive the promised eternal inheritance."*

This free translation highlights the emphasis that is laid on the truth that it is those who have been *called* that receive the promised eternal inheritance. Of course, any emphasis on the *called* does nothing to eclipse the wonderful redemption that Christ accomplished in his death for transgressions under the first covenant as expressed in this passage, but in the original wording the reference to the called is closely linked at the end of the sentence with the eternal inheritance, and this is seen in the context of the writer assuring his readers of the will that Christ has made out for believers.

When a will is being read out in everyday life, those who prove to be beneficiaries have been named in the will and they are therefore destined to gain from it—actually predestined to gain from it. In another sense, they have been *called* according to the will. So it is with the way that Christ has died and brought into effect the benefit of his death. It would be pressing the analogy too much to read into the words of the Hebrews writer a reference to efforts that are made by some in this life to ensure that they "keep sweet" with those who may be coming to the end of their life in order to be a beneficiary, for the way of salvation is such that any beneficiary of Christ's death is one who has been *called*, not one who by efforts has earnt the rights, as it were, to benefit from Christ's will. In translating this passage under discussion, J.B.Phillips rendered "who are called" as " who obey God's call", which amounts to an incorrect view of what the Hebrews writer has in mind in the light of what he says earlier on where he writes of the children that God *gives* to Christ. There is an obedience entailed in being a child of God but it is an obedience that arises from being called initially, and this is why we find our author simply defining us as "those who are called " and not "those who obey God's call."

In many circles this call has been known as an effectual calling. That is to say, it is an internal call experienced by some whereby their governing desires, which are natural and opposed to the will of God, are changed, "giving a new direction to the active powers of the soul, (being) neither resistible nor irresistible, but most free, spontaneous, and yet most certainly effectual" (A.A. Hodge). It is a supernatural call that succeeds in its purpose among those inwardly called.

Many are called externally but never know salvation. Unless there is an inward call, one where the Spirit works mightily in the soul, it will be an ineffectual call. It can be reckoned as ineffectual because of unbelief but, more to the point, it is ineffectual because in the will of God it does not become effective and succeed.

A.A. Hodge observed that God's object is not to destroy but to restore his own work. The called see God's work as restoration and they are glad to see it accomplished in them. In that way they respond to "the heavenly calling" (Heb. 3:1).

Yes, many people experience the external call and it is one that is fleeting in consequence. Not only are the called,

> It is regrettable that the term *irresistible grace* is employed to describe the reason for the call becoming effectual, because it can suggest the called are beckoned to come with them kicking and screaming, as it were, whereas God, one can say, charms them into coming so that freely and spontaneously they are willing to be saved, with them seeing at last that the way of salvation is the better course to follow.

who become inheritors of eternal life, simply described scripturally so often as those who are 'called', but the assumption underlying the nomenclature is that they are defined as such because it is the only call with lasting consequences, and because the Caller cannot fail to find a true response among those chosen for the call. Those singled out for the call will be forever numbered among the called, as the author of Hebrews points out: they are called for an *eternal inheritance*. Nothing can divide them, nor deprive them of that inheritance, as Christ is the mediator of a new covenant. The old covenant was ineffectual, as our author makes clear. The new covenant is an agreement established by God through the redemption Christ accomplished. Christ set out to redeem those whom he already knew to be the called, those who would be effectually won over with their freedom intact as planned.

Owen made much of the New Covenant in his monumental work *The Death of Death*. In Book 3 he begins by opening up on the words of Jeremiah 31:31-2, which words the Hebrews author cites as well. They are fitting words for contemplating the extent of the atonement. Says Owen: ... "the condition of the covenant is not said to be required, but it is absolutely promised: 'I will put my fear in their hearts.'" The promise of an eternal inheritance comes with the certainty of God's purpose being achieved. There is as much certainty, we can say, of some being called as that which saw Christ carry out the act of redemption through his death, for his intent was to set free the called of their transgressions in order to make them eternal inheritors of salvation.

We should also note that just as any privileges of the old covenant only had to do with a few—the lone race of Israel over centuries—so it ought not to be regarded as "scandalous" if the new covenant is not extended universally but only to some, albeit it now embraces Gentiles as well as Jews.

Once more, we draw on the analogy of a prison and the governor's pardon. All prisoners are justly condemned so that if the governor, in not granting a pardon to all but only to those who he calls out to freedom according to his pleasure and by the freedom he exercises according to his authority and even his justice, causes not the guilt of the remaining prisoners to diminish. The called are only inheritors of salvation through God's undeserved mercy.

Redemption in 1 Peter

1 Peter 1:1–2: *"Peter, an apostle of Jesus Christ, To those who are elect exiles of the dispersion in Pontus, Galatia, Cappadocia, Asia, and Bithynia, according to the foreknowledge of God the Father, in the sanctification of the Spirit, for obedience to Jesus Christ and for sprinkling with his blood: May grace and peace be multiplied to you."*

PETER IS ADDRESSING BELIEVING people of Israel who were of the dispersion, which scattered the nation when Babylon sacked Jerusalem. The recipients of Peter's letter were among those who never returned to the land of Israel after the decree of Cyrus the Persian allowed the people to return. While the term *elect* was applied largely without distinction in the Old Testament era to the whole nation, clearly Peter restricts the term in his epistle to those who have become the subjects of God's foreknowledge for salvation in Christ.

One shrewd scholar declares that the Messianic believers (as we call them in our day) were chosen or elected as a group, not as individuals, because Peter is referring to churches of various regions west of Babylon. Doubtless as saved individuals they formed groups in the way of churches, but only because they were all individually elected in the first place. Even if God "visualized" all believers as an elected church in eternity past, they were still viewed as individuals comprising the elected church. And the implication embedded in Peter's benediction is that there were those who were not elect among the exiles of the dispersion. For the term *eklektos* denotes that God chose or selected individuals out (ek-) of many, electing them out of his *free love and wisdom* for their salvation.

Yes, there are those who understand the attribute of God's foreknowledge differently, just as our shrewd scholar does. The actual

91

strength of *eklektos* appears weakened or negated when scholars put forward the thesis that God chose some people out of the mass of mankind on the basis of him merely being able to "predict" that some would come to faith. Even in this way it seems people are saved through God's free love and wisdom, and yet, on the basis that God chooses merely out of prediction, the implication is that the saved have chosen God rather than he choosing them—salvation hinging on the saved having exercised the freedom of their will to choose God so that then God in turn chooses them. It is as Origen put it: "Foreknowledge means no more than seeing what is inside a person."

One would think the act of election—"the choosing of some out of many"—would sufficiently sway all believers into accepting that foreknowledge must by necessity have to do with God knowing beforehand those whom he wishes and wills to save. For we ought to concede that foreknowledge may well mean having foresight as to who will come to faith, but that ability to know beforehand what is likely to happen in God's case must consist of that which is well short of what smacks of predictions that are "wild."

Those who are known as open theists claim that if human choices are "necessary"—so that as choices they are arbitrarily driven by God—then such choices are not "morally significant." Since human choices must be "morally significant", God's foreknowledge cannot be infallible—God is capable of being surprised. Open Theists cite instances from Scripture to demonstrate that God may change his mind ("repent") and not carry out a certain course of punitive action as based on people having changed their mind under a divine threat that appeared to stem from God's fixed determination to bring about disaster out of his holy desire and intent.

Jonathan Edwards in anticipation countered such a notion as propounded by our modern Open Theists by proving from Scripture that God foreknows infallibly human volition, that "necessity" is compatible with "accountability." God knows infallibly what people intend to do as driven by God designing infallibly and sovereignly what he will do. Such infallibility does not dispense with human accountability. If God does not know all things infallibly, foreknowledge becomes conjecture at best. Yet there is no conjecture on his part, as infallible foreknowledge rests on what God intends to do in tandem with human responsibility for our actions, actions that are unable to override his sovereign intentions.

If God does not have what is "exhaustive divine foreknowledge", how do we explain the astounding forecast in Daniel 11 with "its multitude of intricate, human emotions, violitional resolve, and strategic decisions" that all came to pass as prophesied? (See C. Samuel Storms' elucidating essay about Jonathan Edwards on divine knowledge in *The Legacy of Jonathan Edwards*).

It is in the light of election, it is in the light of choosing out from the many certain favored ones who

> Of this we can be assured: God is not ignorant of what he intends to do. If he does not know what he intends to do and actually will do, then his fragile foreknowledge rests on "the incalculable web of human decision making" (C. Samuel Storms), such decision-making that he can be said to be ignorant of.

are to be saved, that foreknowledge, with its certainty of God's will prevailing, is bound to provide a sanctification or a setting apart of the chosen by the Spirit in order that there is a *guaranteed* and *assured* obedience to Jesus Christ, whose blood was bound to be sprinkled to cleanse them. As the original language of Peter has it, the obedience to Christ and the Spirit's sanctification rests by necessity on God's exhaustive knowledge.

If we have any reason to doubt the exhaustiveness of God's knowledge, doubt its infallibility to bring about what he desires as independent of human volition, then recall that Peter proceeds to tell his readers that also foreknown before the foundation of the world was the coming of Jesus so that he would be manifest for we believers in order that our faith and hope may be in God. God's design was bound to succeed with the coming of Christ, as Christ was foreknown to be a "lamb without blemish or spot." Was his spotlessness for sacrifice as necessary for salvation deemed uncertain before he came? He was foreknown as certain to succeed before the world's foundation—not as stemming from bare prediction, but from divine determination and sovereign power.

Redemption in 2 Peter

> 2 Peter 2:1: *"But false prophets also arose from among the people, just as there will be false teachers among you, who will secretly bring in destructible heresies, even denying the Master who bought them, bringing upon themselves swift destruction."*

ADMITTEDLY, THIS IS A difficult passage—as seen to stand alone amidst all the proof that Christ died only for the elect. If there is no reason elsewhere in the New Testament to persuade us that Christ died for all people, then we must reconcile Peter's words with the belief that Christ died and redeemed only those chosen by God. Indeed, we must seek to reconcile it with Peter's own words in his first epistle, in which he states that the elect are destined "for obedience to Jesus Christ and for sprinkling with his blood," inferring that the non-elect are not destined for such, and that therefore Jesus Christ did not die to win their obedience, or to sprinkle them with his blood.

Firstly, it must be established as to whether or not the false teachers, who were bringing in "destructible heresies," were believers. Had they been bought but never redeemed, as one scholar suggests? Another scholar claims that the false teachers had once been true believers, with Peter "charitably (assuming)" they were. Because they were once true believers, the notion is also entertained that herein lies the reason for such vehement condemnation of them by Peter. Another expositor states that such ungodly men will suffer in hell with bitter reproaches because they had actually been bought by Christ.

It has been claimed even by some who contend that Christ died effectually for the elect that the false teachers of the kind that Peter condemns are ungodly though bought by the Master, for such scholars hold to Christ having died efficiently for the elect as well as sufficiently for those not of the elect.

This means the problem posed by Peter's words will be wrestled over much and prove to be particularly thorny for any who insist that Christ at least died efficiently for the elect. McDonald is one scholar who believes in the sovereign of God for eternal salvation but speaks of people being bought without being redeemed, being "purchased" without being saved.

One wonders if Christ can be said to have bought people but not redeemed them, how he purchased them at great cost with his blood but not rescued them! If we hold that Christ died only for the elect, then we are relieved of such illogicality and contradiction. And yet we are left wrestling with what the apostle means when he describes those who are unrighteous and are kept under punishment until the Day of Judgment (v.9)—ones who are said to have been bought by the Master, only to deny him.

Turretin, in answering detractors in his day, said that Peter meant by "bought" a "deliverance from error and idolatry", "a deliverance effected by an outward exhibition of the Gospel, and a setting apart for the ministry." He goes on to state that Christ had called the false teachers into the Church, into the house he owns as Master. Turretin contends that Peter is careful to use the word 'Master', not 'Savior'. Some scholars bring in a Trojan horse by referring to the false teachers as being 'bought' and therefore by necessity "redeemed", therefore Turretin, in the light of his definition of "bought", may be seen making a sound point in refuting the notion that men could be bought without being redeemed. And then, sound exegete as he was, Turretin reminds us of the words Peter employs further into his letter—

> "For if, after they have escaped the defilements of the world through the knowledge of our Lord and Savior Jesus Christ, they are again entangled in them and overcome, the last state has become worse for them than the first."
>
> For it would have been better for them never to have known the way of righteousness than after knowing it to have turned back from the holy commandment delivered to them. What the true proverb says has happened to

them: *'The dog returns to its own vomit, and the sow, after washing itself, returns to wallow in the mire'."*

The Reformer says that a knowledge of our Lord and Savior, and knowing the way of righteousness, translates here into a mere "deliverance from pagan errors and idolatries, and to a calling of the knowledge of the truth." In this way they denied their Master.

Yet, if their denial of the Master who bought them appears no different from the denial of any other unbeliever, then the false teachers' conduct was not especially wicked. Why was it particularly wicked, as underscored by a particularly scathing judgement by the apostle? It became such because they were called to a knowledge of our Lord and Savior and made themselves teachers. The denial was expressed in false teaching. Turretin quotes from Hebrews 10:29 to show that there is a work of *external* sanctification in terms of the blood of the Covenant made with Christ, as opposed to a genuine sanctification that is *internal*.

Owen, the author of *Death of Death*, maintains it is uncertain as to whether it is stated that the false teachers were bought by the Master in reality, or if on the other hand the false teachers understood or presumed it to be so.

In elaborating on the words of Peter, Owen shows that it is certain that no fruit of righteousness is said to have been evidenced in the false teachers' lives, only that they had "common gifts and knowledge", gifts and knowledge that many are acquainted with, even though Christ did not actually purchase them with his blood.

Owen claims that whenever the Scriptures speak of the redemption of God's people, more endearing names for the Purchaser are used, such as Christ and Lord. The appellation "Master" is not usually used "if at all of Christ but for God the Father."

As for the word "bought", the Reformer views it as one describing any kind of deliverance, the Old Testament bearing witness to this. For Owen to speak of the Old Testament is apt since Peter compares the false teachers with the false prophets of old. Therefore, the "buying" of the false teachers was restricted to a knowledge that allowed them to escape the world's defilements, and not to the actual purchase of them by Christ's blood. On the purchasing of them by Christ's blood Peter is silent. Only a certain deliverance is mentioned, not an actual purchase by blood. Owen likens the situation to that of King Ahaz believing that the gods of the kings of Syria helped him when actually he "sacrificed to the gods of Damascus that had defeated him" (2 Chron. 28:23). Like King Ahaz who had a false opinion, the false teachers had a false opinion concerning the Master's purchase, Ahaz reckoning that the gods of Damascus had helped him when they had not.

Some other points can also be considered.

One, it is safe to assume that the false teachers and the false Old Testament prophets were alike in their rejection of the truth. It is never stated in the Old Testament that the false prophets fell away from belief, that they were lapsed believers. As a corollary, we can conclude that the New Testament false teachers also were not lapsed believers. Also, that they are said to bring in destructive heresies may lend itself to the thought that they brought themselves into the church with the heresies, as those coming into the congregations from outside them, not having been believers and of the congregations in the first place.

> To drive home the truth that Christ died only for the elect, Owen says also that it can be no more said that the false teachers were actually bought by Christ's blood than to say that Christ died for those who will never hear of Christ.

Two, so as to endorse the fact that the false teachers were never believers but merely considered themselves to be, the proverb that Peter quotes in support of the false teachers' evil shows that the pretenders were always dogs, were always pigs (v.22). George Lawson in his Exposition of Proverbs says of the proverb to do with the dog—the one to do with the pig is extra-biblical—that the dog tells us of people whose "weakened consciences resist sin; but their love to it is not diminished; and for the most part their corruptions obtain the victory over their consciences, and they return

> The proverb of the pig underlines even more that the impostors were never actually purchased by the blood of Christ: Despite washing itself, the sow remains a sow. All the time the false teachers had been pigs—washed but returning to wallow in the mud once again. All along they were dogs—now going back to their vomit.

to their former kind of life with redoubled eagerness." Therefore, we may add that in the case of the false teachers, their evil eagerness redoubled in becoming teachers who then hoped more than ever to bring down true believers.

The false teachers, despite a washing, were never inwardly washed. Were they not bought but not purchased? It is a contradiction in terms. It is truer to conclude that they considered themselves bought. Their lives proved they had not been purchased.

The kind of knowledge that the false teachers acquired also differs from that which Peter speaks about at the beginning of his letter when he seeks to assure his readers (who are true believers) of the salvation that is theirs in Christ. He writes to those who had obtained a faith of equal standing with that of the apostles by the righteousness of our God and Savior Jesus Christ, that is, Peter's readers had been given a faith of equal value to that of the apostles. Michael Green states that the word for "equal standing" is a political word, signifying "the amnesty of the king." We always do well to remind ourselves that Christ stands for King, therefore it is apt to contemplate that we who are of faith receive a pardon from King Jesus, whose righteousness secured it. In this way the pardon is deemed "precious." The preciousness of such a faith is enhanced at the thought of it being *obtained*, received by lot, received through divine allotment (see Strong's Exhaustive Concordance of the Bible).

J.B. Phillips sums it up well in his translation: " . . . to those who have been given a faith as valuable as ours in the righteousness of our God, and savior Jesus Christ." (An excellent translation, except there is considerable justification for accepting grammatically the two nouns of 'God' and 'savior' as referring to Christ).

Now, if salvation and redemption has as its contingent the giving of faith (and not merely the offer to place faith in Christ), then it is absurd to consider the false teachers as ones having been bought in reality by Christ. Obviously, the false teachers were not given such faith of equal standing with the apostles, not having been given an amnesty from the King. Not all are given faith, such a faith that is born out of the righteousness of our God and Savior

Jesus Christ—a faith that is just as certain as the evident righteousness of Christ.

Peter speaks of both his believing readers and the false teachers as having *knowledge*, except that the believing-readers' knowledge, unlike that of the false teachers, is accompanied by divine power that grants "all things that pertain to life and godliness", which arises from the readers having been effectually *called*, and having been given divine promises to be partakers of the divine nature (1:1–4).

The false teachers are also said to have escaped the defilements of the world, but only for a time. Soon they are entangled in the defilements of the world. On the other hand, Peter's readers are bound to remain free of the entanglements of the world's corruption because: 1. They have been given a precious faith, 2. Divine power is theirs for life and godliness, 3. Precious and great promises ensure it will be so, 4. They are called effectually for God's glory and excellence, just as Peter says (1:3).

Peter could not write that way when speaking of the false teachers, as they were merely washed pigs—pigs from the start.

Redemption in 1 John

1 John 2:2: *"He is the propiation for our sins, and not for ours only, but also for the sins of the whole world"*

JOHN OWEN, THE RENOWNED Puritan, in his monumental work *Death of Death* passes through with reasonable examination a large number of scriptural texts that have been appealed to in support of universal redemption, but the above text is one to which he devotes special attention because he believed it 'is urged (by universalists) with most confidence and pressed with most importunity'.

With finely-tuned argumentation Owen marshals the following points (to put it simply and not necessarily point by sequential point as Owen has it) :1. Although John's epistle does not directly define the identity of the recipients, we know John was an apostle to the Jews and writes to those of a kind that first became acquainted with the gospel, viz. the Jews, 2. John was conscious of belonging to that race of God's first choice, "in opposition to the residue of believers in the world (Gentiles)", 3. John's hearers formerly hated the Gentiles and needed to be reminded that there were now believing Gentiles whose sins had been forgiven in Christ, 4. John writes to comfort his hearers, who would find no comfort in believing "Christ died for an innumerable that shall be damned," 5. Christ can hardly be said to be a propitiation and advocate of all in the world, thus satisfying and pacifying God for the sake of those who will not become reconciled to him, 6. The term "the whole world" is not infrequently used in a restrictive sense in many places in Scripture.

Owen then briefly answers two objections. One has to do with the notion that John is seeking to comfort everyone in the world who may have doubts and fears. Owen merely states that he has made it clear that John's words of comfort are restricted to believers. The second objection belongs to the claim that "our sins" are those of believers, while "the sins of the whole world" are the sins of any who are not believers but make up the rest of the whole world. Owen contends that "our sins" are those of Jewish believers, while "the sins of the whole world" are those of believing Gentiles. Or, it is possible, says he, that "our sins" were of all those—Jew and Gentile—who were contemporaries of John, and "the sins of the whole world" are to be of the believers of succeeding years. Yet Owen is more convinced that the Jewish-Gentiles paradigm is the most likely explanation.

As for Turretin, he argues that Christ is only a propitiation for believers, his position being quite identical to Owen's in elucidating our text by showing Christ is both propitiator and advocate, and in two such offices—offices inseparable—he cannot be said to be a comfort for those who are unbelievers. It is no comfort for believers to think that propitiation and advocacy is common to those who have no saving faith.

Turretin, like Owen, entertains the notion that John could be referring to the sins of all contemporary believers and then to those of believers in succeeding ages, saying it is of "little moment" whether it is a Jewish-Gentile paradigm or a contemporary-future one. He says this in the light of the epistles being commonly called "catholic epistles"—forming much of the end of the New Testament, and are epistles addressing any believers the world over to their comfort.

Still, we must say that while such epistles were dubbed "catholic" or "general" from early days because it was held that they were letters addressed not to specific churches or individuals, a more accurate description of such epistles ought to be "Jewish epistles." The final letters of the New Testament were penned by Jewish authors and were for Messianic Jews; therefore it is of some moment that this is recognized. They are unlike the letters penned by Paul who was a missioner to the Gentiles. It is true that there were Jewish recipients of his letters, as Romans in particular makes plain, but they were written for the most part by Paul to assure the Gentiles that they also were in the fold of God's flock, alongside those who belonged to the race that had alone been favored by God in a singular way in times past. On the other hand, the letters penned for a

Jewish audience came with the reminder that Gentile believers were accepted on equal footing with those who were privileged to be the first to hear the gospel and believe. That reminder is not frequently found in the "Jewish epistles," but it is there when it is deemed necessary to sound it out.

Even Revelation is essentially a Jewish book, so that all the writings in the New Testament canon from Hebrews on definitely must have been placed together at the end of the New Testament because they are Jewish in origin and flavor. Even though church historians do not hint at this, it is easy to see from the evidence of the New Testament itself that the still-existing privileges of God's ancient people were widely recognized in the Early Church, and respect was paid to the outstanding enlightment Messianic Jewish apostles and leaders possessed, hence the Jewish epistles quickly gained a wider audience than first intended for the sake of the welfare of Gentile churches as well.

Owen's argument for the Jewish-Gentile paradigm is convincing if we should ask: "What drove John to point out that Jesus died for the sins of the whole world also?" We can well imagine how Jewish believers could have become smug when John wrote so *assuredly* that Jesus was their advocate and propitiator as those of God's ancient people; those first to receive the gospel, and in the belief that the gospel was solely for them; as those who personally knew that someone of their race (John) was there in the very beginning and saw, heard and touched the word of life. John felt compelled to remind them that Jesus had sheep among the Gentiles as well (John 10:16, as penned by the same author of 1 John).

> It is too easy to forget that 1 John, for instance, is Jewish in origin, and was originally sent by John to Jewish brethren, too easy to forget it because Gentiles form in our time the dominant numbers in the Christian Church, as they have now done for centuries. Yet, if we recall that the likes of Jews, such as John, saw, heard, and touched the word of life in the beginning (1:1–4) because they were of the privileged race of Israel, and then realise that the privileged and believing ones of that race needed to be reminded that Jesus died not only for them but for believing Gentiles as well, we can understand why John penned the words about Jesus being not merely the advocate and the propitiator for the sins of his fellow Jews but for Gentiles too.

Some Reformed scholars in the seventeenth century had read into John's words that the apostle means that Christ's act of propitiation was efficient for the elect and sufficient for those not elected. This was not the thinking of the likes of Owen and Turretin. We saw earlier (for instance, see notes under John 6:33), when we observed that it was the view commonly shared among the delegates at the Synod of Dort in the Netherlands in 1618–19. If there is ever a desire to draw up a basis for belief among those who hold to election, it may appear to be a happy compromise to allow room for holding to a doctrine of Christ's death being sufficient for those not of the elect. Yet, while tolerance is to be championed among those who believe in election and who differ on the question of whether or not there is a sufficiency in Christ's death for the non-elect, we need to ask whether or not John's words—or other apostolic words in the rest of the New Testament—suggest such a notion.

(It may be odd that many who have a sincere heart for the salvation of Jewish people often neglect the Jewish viewpoint of the New Testament. Yet, such is the desire to seize upon texts that seem to support a doctrine that Christ's death was for the individuals of every nation, that the Jewish perspective is not contemplated—such is the determination to champion the dogma of so-called "free will" so that the efficacy of the atonement hangs on human choice rather than God's grace and his prerogative to forgive or not).

It appears that the Synod of Dort never considered the Jewish perspective when weighing up the extent of Christ's atonement, but would it have made any difference if the Synod had? Judging on Owen's defence of the doctrine that Christ died for the sins of the elect alone, it would have made a definite difference, for in the consideration of Jewish perspective Owen was persuaded that the Jewish perspective finds the meaning of "sins of the whole world" can be nothing else but the sins of other believers in Gentiles.

Of course, it was not the Jewish viewpoint alone that caused Owen to interpret "for the sins of the whole world" to mean the sins of believing Gentiles. While such a viewpoint served well to dismiss a commonly accepted notion of a universality of Christ's redemption, Owen buttresses his defense of what may be unfortunately known as "limited atonement" with a fine, defensible exposition of what must be really understood of propitiation and advocacy, showing that such redeeming features are twin acts and were of a kind that made effectual the design for the salvation of only those actually reconciled to God the Father. If Christ pacified the wrath of God through propitiation, if he satisfied God with his sacrifice so as to secure *advocacy* as well, why are unbelievers condemned? Has Christ not already paid the price for their sins and intercedes effectually for them as their advocate too?

Such deduction led Owen to counter the teaching that was held by the likes of Richard Baxter, who ventured to state that God sent his Son to die for all people, except that the blessing of it was suspended upon people believing to their salvation—this Baxter claimed even though he was an exponent of sovereign grace for the elect's salvation. While holding to the tenet that God in his sovereign will only gives effectual grace to the elect so that they are saved, Baxter nevertheless believed Christ died even for those non-elect on the assumption that God had foreseen that no person in their natural state would believe, and/but despite any inability, God decreed to choose some who would inevitably believe and secure their salvation. God desired that all be saved, hence Christ died for all, said Baxter in effect. So much for propitiation, and what of Christ's advocacy? Did Christ die in vain and is he an advocate in vain? Somehow, Baxter seemed to think that Christ's propitiation and advocacy was not in vain because he maintained that all do not believe, as it is not in God's sovereign will for them to believe! Such a universalism as touching on Christ's death has come to be known as Ideal or Hypothetical.

It is difficult to think that when John wrote that Christ is the propitiation for the sins of the whole world, he had in mind a hypothetical notion of it. Otherwise, it means that for John those of the whole world, (as Baxter understood it) had as much of the propitiation and advocacy that Christ accomplished through His death as the believers to whom John wrote!

It may seem spiritual and lofty to state that Christ's majesty was of the greatest dimension in dying for all men, that he was acknowledging the dignity of all men, but it actually undercuts his majesty to imagine that it was the divine will to save all but actually not to save all. When one contemplates the enormous cost Christ underwent on the cross, it constitutes "a kind of divine extravagance" (as someone has described it) to go to extraordinary lengths to save all but be powerless to save all.

Even if Christ has died just for the elect, the glory of the atonement is far from being diminished on that account. The fact is that such a redemption accomplishes its purpose and could not fail brings forth glory and praise. For one thing, as John Murray observed, "Every nation and kindred and people and tongue is . . . embraced in the propitiation." Murray also said: "The utmost bounds of human need and the utmost bounds of divine grace know no other propitiation—it is for the whole world." The apostle is also stressing in our text the perpetuity of Jesus' sacrifice—it is effectual "for the ever-recurring and ever-continuing sins of believers" (Murray again). Such a grand design lay behind Jesus' sacrifice that it is demeaning to regard such a grand purpose of his becoming thwarted by human unbelief.

As Owen, Turretin and Murray note: 1 John is a Jewish letter that speaks of advocacy as well as propitiation. Turretin notes in regard to this that "Christ is not an advocate for all." Clearly he was for the believing people of his own race an advocate, as even the name "Christ" signifies he is the king of Israel at least. John seeks to assure believing Gentiles that they are also under the intercessory sway of that kingship too. The Gentiles are assured that Jesus is both advocate and propitiator for them. The propitiation does not have an extent far beyond Jesus' advocacy, that is, Jesus is not a hopeful and uncertain propitiator as contingent on so-called 'free-will' on one hand, and on the other hand a certain advocate for the believing. Advocacy and propitiation go hand in hand in the certainty of Christ's work succeeding.

So we see that the Jewish perspective plays a formidable part in revealing "Christ missed (not) his aim and shed His blood in vain" (Turretin). He proved himself not merely to be a worthy substitute for the believing among his own people, but for the believing beyond his own ethnic race so that redemption in that sense has come to the whole world.

Redemption in Revelation

> Revelation 13:18: ... "*and all who dwell on earth will worship (the Beast), everyone whose name has not been found written before the foundation of the world in the book of life of the Lamb that was slain*" (ESV).

TRANSLATIONS OF THE TEXT have varied between "all whose names have been written in the book of life belonging to the Lamb that was slain from the foundation of the world" (NIV) and that above (ESV). There has been debate over the text because it is grammatically possible that "before the foundation of the world" can modify either "written" (as in the ESV), or "slain" (as in the NIV). The NIV provides a footnote to Rev.13:8, showing that an alternative reading is: ... "written from the creation of the world in the book of life belonging to the Lamb that was slain", thus favoring as the main text the wording that speaks of our names being in the book of life that belongs to the Lamb who was slain before the foundation of the world.

The translators of the NIV need not be seen as showing doctrinal bias, for it can be asserted that what forms the footnote and appears as the subtext does not follow the word order found in the original language. Neither is the footnote to be regarded necessarily as inferior, for the footnote is prefaced with "or." Bruce Metzger's *A Textual Commentary on the Greek New Testament (Second Edition)* has no

---

Not a few are willing to wed the truth of the slaying of the Lamb before the foundation of the world with the thought of names of the eternally saved having been written in the book of life before the world was formed. Still, if the plan for the Lamb being slain was formed before the world began, God must have had in mind all those who would benefit to their salvation in the slain Lamb at the same time. The Lamb was not destined to be slain in vain. The whole plan of salvation was a *fait accompli* from eternity.

critical note on this passage under discussion, cursorily suggesting that the grammatical issue is open to the modifier either being "written" or "slain", though Metzer has been among editors of the Greek New Testament who subscribe to the main text being that which sees the Lamb as the subject of predestination before the foundation of the world.

Perhaps it is just as the author has observed about some other so-called disputed passages in Scripture, that the text has been divinely preserved with a double meaning in view: Thus our text may convey the truth that the Lamb was slain before the foundation of the world and also that there are those whose names were written in the book of life before the world's foundation. The NIV's main text runs with the word order of the original, therefore it is most likely that in this passage it is the Lamb who is in mind when John speaks about the time prior to the world's formation. It seems that it is merely because 17:8 refers to unbelievers whose names are not written in the book of life from eternity that not a few translators (such as those of the ESV) have leant towards the modifier in 13:8 being "written" and not "slain."

Yet, Lenski desires us to see that while he contends that 13:8 has in view the Lamb having been slain before the foundation of the world, he reminds us that God " elected us in connection with (Christ) before the foundation of the world", so that we may turn our thoughts to synthesizing 13:8 and 17:8. One cannot help seeing that in such a synthesis the twin truths of the Lamb being slain before the world's formation and believers also having their names written in the book of life (the book of life that *belongs* to the Lamb, as the wording of the NIV indicates) before the world's formation, then believers' certainty of salvation is no less certain than Christ having been foreordained to be slain.

Theologically, it is plausible to hold that the Lamb was slain before the foundation of the world—this is regarded as orthodox doctrine. Yet, not all believers readily accept the view that the saved have their names written before the foundation of the world in the book of life. While some, as believers in the doctrine of predestination, accept our names have been written before the foundation of the world in the book of life and will never be erased from that book, others, who do not hold to the doctrine of God's sovereignty in salvation in its classic sense, may accept that our names may be in the book of life before we are born but that they may be blotted out of the book due to apostasy and to the loss of our salvation.

Yet, the certainty of salvation for those whose names are in the book from eternity lies as well in learning that with the rise of the Antichrist everyone whose name is in the book of life will not worship that Beast. Mc Donald is correct in stating: ..."because (those whose names have not been written in the book of life) are not found among the redeemed, they are given over to error." Even if one favors the translation of Rev.13:8 applying to the Lamb having been slain before the foundation of the world, there is no doubt that Rev.17:8 affirms that there are those whose names have been inscribed in the book of life before the world's formation and who will not become spellbound by the demonic force of the Beast. There is nothing to suggest that people may have their names in the book of life and then fall away into apostasy to the loss of their salvation. On the contrary, even when the forces of evil will be at their worst just prior to the return of Christ, true and predestined believers will be found withstanding those most hostile and bewitching forces. And it has more than God's foreknowledge or power to do than to predict what is to occur—meaning that God has more than predicted or guessed who will be saved. As certain as it was for the Lamb to be slain, as certain as there were people whose names were in the book of life before the world was made, it is certain that those redeemed will not be given over to error but come through victorious.

And John, who writes in Revelation about the Lamb, writes of him who takes away the sin of the world according to what he also wrote in his Gospel. The sin of every human being? As we established in looking at John 1:29, the redemption is in mind there of Jew and Gentile, who as two races formed the world in Jewish eyes. Yet, here in Revelation, as he does in his Gospel, John reveals a further qualification than that of Jew and Gentile—a more definite one as touching on the foreordination of certain ones for eternal life, be they Jew or Gentile. And in this light, it is difficult to conceive that if Christ died for those whose names were not written down before the world was created, that he would even die a sufficient but not efficient death for all. Clearly, his death was alone efficient, his sacrifice as the Lamb effectual for the elect.

What a great comfort to know that one has been destined for eternal life, particularly will it be so when such a severe trial as that under the dreaded Antichrist eventuates! The Lamb will preserve his own people come-what-may, though some may cast doubt on the certainty of such endurance when they note that the apostle must resort to a warning in the light of the Antichrist appearing—

> It is inconceivable that the foreknowledge of God and of Christ was subject to conjecture when having in mind the redemption of mankind. So divinely certain were the outcome to choose many for salvation that Christ came ready as the Lamb—the names of the elect written down long beforehand. God foreknows all because he foreordains all things, pace Open Theism.

> "If anyone has an ear, let him hear:
> If anyone is to be taken captive,
> to captivity he goes;
> if an anyone is to be slain with the sword,
> with the sword he must be slain.
> Here is a call for the endurance and faith for the saints"
> (Revelation 13:9, 10).

God's people are prophetically called on to endure and to have faith, but they can afford to be exhorted to endure, since they are sensitive to the need—unlike those who will be so entranced with the Antichrist that they are doomed to suffer the wrath of God.

It appears a contradiction that the elect must be warned to endure and have faith, and also seems to be so when it is regarded to be a great incentive for the elect to preach the eternal gospel (Revelation 14:6), even when it seems all hope is lost in seeing any more people saved as the perilous times of the Antichrist set in but, knowing that even when the midnight hour approaches, if there are any still left of those whose names are written in the Lamb's book, they are bound to be saved. Be they Jew or Gentile, they will be saved.

Conclusion

IT MAY SMACK OF scholasticism that one reaches for an analogy in the world's prison system and in the prerogative of an authority to grant a pardon and a release from prison for anyone the authority chooses, that is, without questioning the right of the authority to use his freedom to do so. Such an analogy may seem to be countered with the assertion that the New Testament Scriptures make it plain that the promise to release any prisoner of sin is for all mankind without exception. Do not the Scriptures make plain that Christ died for all without exception?

The analogy of the right of a secular authority to release any prisoner at his own pleasure as it bears on divine forgiveness is valid because the Scriptures do speak of sinners being prisoners of sin and how it is the pleasure of God on which hinges the release and forgiveness of any. Paul's opening words in Ephesians keep stressing that the saved are redeemed according to the will and pleasure of God. Galatians alerts us to the fact that we were held captive under the law until Christ came.

Our task is to reconcile what is depicted as bondage to sin with the apparent universality implied in Christ's death. Classic Universalists appear logical in their claim that all mankind are to be redeemed by Christ's sacrifice—

A. All mankind is under the bondage of sin

B. Christ died to redeem all mankind from the bondage of sin

C. Therefore, all mankind is redeemed

Classic universalists acknowledge to their credit that redemption means redemption, that Christ's death was for effectual redemption since we could not save ourselves (for we all were under

CONCLUSION

the bondage of sin), but we must question the minor premise: Did in fact Christ die to redeem all mankind?

In the pursuit of an adequate solution to what seems a universality of redemption, it is necessary to define what is meant by such terms as "all" and "the world", whenever the Scriptures relate those terms to redemption through the cross.

We have seen that particularity in the form of the election of Israel as the sole beneficiary of God's revelation before Christ means that no surprise is necessarily sprung on us in learning that the adoption of election also runs as a precious thread in the New Testament age, with God still free and acting out of sovereign grace, having elected those whom he willed to be saved through the redemption of Christ.

It can be demonstrated from the New Testament Scriptures that the common call in evangelism lay in the need for hearers merely to believe the promise that Christ died for sinners. Never was there an appeal of "Christ died for you," simply because no one can be certain that Christ died for them until he or she believes the promise on the grounds that Christ died for sinners such as them, and then are divinely moved to exercise faith in Christ, and so to learn that he died at least effectually for them.

Over and over again such terms as "all," "the world" and "the whole world" can simply be reduced to mean that Christ died for Gentiles as well as Jews. Since almost the whole of the New Testament was written by Jews and therefore from their perspective, such is to is to be taken into account.

When this viewpoint is taken empathetically, it can help us to cut through what needs to be qualified so that we see that not all men know what it is to die to sin and live for Christ, who only died for those who die to sin and live by his resurrecting power.

George Herbert, the great English devotional poet, penned some vivid verse about the grim resolve to obey God's "strict decree" to love him with all his heart, only he was told by someone that it was impossible to do so. What could he do? He said he would *trust* in God "to be my light." To trust in God? He was told that only God could enable him to trust. Nothing can be done on our part, this we must confess. Yet, it is not even ours to confess! This amazed him. It troubled him to think he could not contribute a thing to his salvation. Yet a friend calmed him by assuring him that "all things were more ours by being his." All had been forfeited through Adam. All now relies on Christ "Who cannot fail or fall." Yes, all things are more ours by being his.

The Holdfast

I threatened to observe the strict decree
    Of my dear God with all my power and might.
    But I was told by one, it could not be;
Yet I might trust God to be my light.

Then will I trust, said I, in him alone.
    Nay, even to trust him, was also his:
    We must confess, that nothing is our own.
Then I confess that he my succor is:

But to have naught is ours, not to confess
    That we have nought. I stood amazed at this,
    Much troubled, till I heard a friend express,
That all things were more ours by being his.
    What Adam had, and forfeited for all,
    Christ keepeth now, who cannot fail or fall.

Bibliography

Ralph H. Alexander, *The Expositor's Bible Commentary—Ezekiel*

Bauer, Arndt, Gingrich, *A Greek Lexicon of the New Testament*

Darrell L. Bock, *The NIV Application Commentary—Luke* (Zondervan)

F. F. Bruce, *Romans* (Tyndale)

Don Carson, *The Gospel According to John* (Eerdmans)

Alan Cole, *Exodus—Commentary* (Tyndale Press)

Custance, *The Sovereignty of Grace*

E. Earle Ellis, *The Century Bible—Luke* (Nelson, 1966)

Godet, *Commentary on Luke* (Kregel, 1981)

Thomas Goodwin, *Justifying Faith* (Vol.8, Banner of Truth)

William Hendriksen, *New Testament Commentary—Matthew* (Banner of Truth)

William Hendriksen, *New Testament Commentary—Luke* (Banner of Truth)

A. A. Hodge, *Outlines of Theology* (Banner of Truth)

P. E. Hughes, *Paul's Second Epistle to the Corinthians* (Marshal, Morgan & Scott, 1962)

Jamieson, Fausett, Brown, *A Commentary* (Vol 3, Eerdmans)

George Lawson, *Exposition of Proverbs*

Lenski, *The Interpretation of Matthew's Gospel* (Ausburg Pub House, 1964)

Lenski, *The Interpretation of Mark's Gospel* (Ausburg Pub House, 1964)

Lenski, *St John's Revelation* (Ausburg Pub House, 1964)

R. H. Lightfoot, *St John's Gospel* (Oxford Paperbacks, 1960)

BIBLIOGRAPHY

William McDonald, *Believer's Bible Commentary* (Nelson, 1989)

Alva McLain, *Romans* (1980)

Eugene Merrill, *Kingdom of Priests* (Baker, 2000)

Bruce Metzger, *A Textual Commentary of the New Testament* (Second Edition, German Bible Society)

Leon Morris, *Luke* (IVP, 1974)

C.F.D. Moule, *The Cambridge Bible Commentary*—Mark (C'b Univ Press)

Newberry, *The Englishman's Greek New Testament* (Zondervan, 1978)

John Owen, *The Death of Christ* (B of T edition, Vol 10)

J. I. Packer, *Introductory Essay to John Owen's Death of Death* (monograph)

David Pawson, *Israel in the New Testament*

J. B. Phillips, *The New Testament in Modern English*

Arthur Pink, *The Sovereignty of God* (Bridge-Logos, 2008)

Psalter Hymnal, *Doctrinal Standards . . . of the Christian Reformed Church—containing The Canons of Dort* (Reformed Church Publishers, Michigan, 1934)

Reader's Digest, *A Modern Guide to Synonyms*

J. C. Ryle, *Expository Thoughts on John* (B of T edition, 1987)

Saphir, *Epistle to the Hebrews*

Stein, *The New American Commentary*—Luke (Broadman)

David H Stern, *Jewish New Testament Commentary* (JNTP, 1992)

David H Stern, *The Complete Jewish Bible* (JNTP, 1998)

Francis Turretin, *The Atonement of Christ* (Baker, 1978)

United Bible Society, *The Greek New Testament* (Third Edition)

Westcott, *Westcott's St John* (James Clarke & Co., 1958)

Westminster Theological Journal, *The Extent of the Atonement —at the Synod of Dort* (Spring 1989, Vol 51, Nos 1 and 2)

Witherington 111, *Letters and Homilies for Helenized Christians*

Witherington 111, *Letters and Homilies for Jewish Christians*

www.ingramcontent.com/pod-product-compliance
Lightning Source LLC
Chambersburg PA
CBHW070922160426
43193CB00011B/1554